ÉDITH

FIND ME A NEW WAY TO DIE

PIAF

THE UNTOLD STORY

DAVID BRET

ÉDITH

FIND ME A NEW WAY TO DIE

PIAF

THE UNTOLD STORY

OBERON BOOKS
LONDON

WWW.OBERONBOOKS.COM

First published in 2015 by Oberon Books Ltd

521 Caledonian Road, London N7 9RH

Tel: +44 (0) 20 7607 3637

Fax: +44 (0) 20 7607 3629

e-mail: info@oberonbooks.com

www.oberonbooks.com

A catalogue record for this book is available from the British Library.

HB ISBN: 978-1-78319-929-7

E ISBN: 978-1-78319-928-0

Printed and bound by Replika Press Pvt. Ltd., India.

Visit www.oberonbooks.com to read more about all our books and to buy them. You will also find features, author interviews and news of any author events, and you can sign up for e-newsletters so that you're always first to hear about our new releases.

This book is dedicated to Barbara (1930-97),
the greatest chanteuse of the modern age—and to
Joey Stefano (1968-94) and Les Enfants de Novembre.

N'oublie pas...

La vie sans amis c'est comme

Un jardin sans fleurs.

Acknowledgements

■　　■　　■

Writing this book would not have been possible had it not been for the inspiration, criticisms and love of that select group of individuals whom I have always regarded as my true family and autre coeur: Barbara, Marlene Dietrich, Dorothy Squires, Roger Normand, Irene Bevan, René and Lucette Chevalier, Jacqueline Danno, Annick Roux, Joey Stefano, Hélène Delavault, Terry Sanderson, Betty and Gérard Gamain, John and Anne Taylor, Charley Marouani, Francois and Madeleine Vals. Most of you are gone, but will live on in my heart.

Un grand chapeau-bas for Louis Dupont, Fernand Lumbruso, François Bellair, Sylvie Galthier, Damia, Michel Émer, Manouche, Serge Reggiani, Marcel Blistene, Caroline Clerc, Charles Aznavour, Charles Dumont, Catherine Jan, Simone Margantin, Betty Mars, Claude Sounac, Peggy Lee, Elisabeth Welch, Simone Berteaut, Madame Leclerc.

And lastly my grateful thanks to the wonderful team at Oberon.

Preface

■   ■   ■

The French music-hall has always fascinated me. I grew up with it, and in 1988 published my first book on the subject, *The Piaf Legend*. This I followed with biographies of Maurice Chevalier and Mistinguett, and in 1998, for the twenty-fifth anniversary of her death, I published *Piaf: A Passionate Life*. Many of my friends, past and present, are connected to the chanson one way or another. Barbara, the greatest singer in France since Piaf, was one of my closest friends. So too were Marlene Dietrich, Roger Normand, Dorothy Squires and several others in this volume. Over the course of my career I have also been fortunate to have known many of those who knew and worked with Piaf, some sadly no longer with us, who were happy to share their anecdotes with me. Now, in celebration of her centenary, I have assembled these interviews with friends, lovers, colleagues and songwriters. They tell Piaf's story as it has never been told before.

Contents

Introduction

■   ■   ■

It was Dorothy Squires who suggested, back in 1986, that I write a book about Édith Piaf. I had grown up listening to her songs, I owned every recording she had ever made, I had boxes of newspaper clippings—I guess you could say that I was obsessed. So I wrote the book, Dorothy read through the script, and I sent it off to my agent. By then I had met some of the people interviewed in this current book: Louis Dupont, the father of what was then thought to be Piaf's only child; her astrologer, Catherine Jan; Madame Leclerc, who looked after her grave in the Père Lachaise cemetery; her songwriter, Michel Émer; Damia, the biggest singer in France pre-Piaf … and Barbara, regarded by many as not just Piaf's successor, but her equal. In 1988, I published *The Piaf Legend*, a brief tome which told the basic story of 'The Little Sparrow'. Five years later, to coincide with the biopic, *La Môme* (UK: *La Vie en Rose*), I published a much larger study, *Piaf: A Passionate Life*. In this I included parts of interviews that I had conducted with a number of Piaf's friends, lovers, songwriters and other acquaintances, some of whom by now had become close personal friends. I was also privileged to encounter Simone Berteaut, who claimed in her very famous book to have been Piaf's half-sister. Mômone, as she was nicknamed, was a *very* strange lady who during our meeting still maintained that essential blood connection, whilst declaring that Piaf's other siblings were impostors. There is of course no way of knowing. Piaf's father, Louis Gassion, is said to have fathered nineteen children—what is strange is that only three of these ever came forward, and only then when (according to Mômone) they needed something.

Certain conditions were imposed by some of those that I spoke to. Marlene Dietrich did not mind what I wrote. She was a close friend of both Piaf and myself, and always spoke her mind—too much so, at times, which is why much of what she said about Piaf is now being divulged for the first time, having been removed from my previous books. Marlene had a very dry sense of humour, and her tales of what happened when she and Piaf attended parties in Hollywood are hilarious. Similarly, Louis Dupont's revelations about Louis Leplée, the drag-queen impresario who discovered Piaf, were to a certain extent suppressed, along with observations made by Irene Bevan—Gracie Fields' stepdaughter who worked for Piaf's first *husband*, Jacques Pills—and by Manouche, the celebrated gangster's moll who was a frequent visitor to Piaf's apartment (in a brothel) during World War II. Serge Reggiani, who worked with Piaf in her first major film and went on to become one of the most feted singers in France, did not wish for his revelations to be published during his lifetime—likewise Simone Margantin, Piaf's last nurse who probably saw and heard more than she should have while in her employ, after Piaf's marriage to Théo Sarapo.

My godparents, Roger Normand and Jacqueline Danno, knew Piaf well—Roger from the 1940s, Jacqueline during the last year of her life. Michel Émer, Charles Aznavour and Charles Dumont were amongst her favourite songwriters, and were witness to both sides of her—the loving, benevolent woman who could turn into a tyrant at the drop of a hat if she was not getting her own way. It was Aznavour who gave my publisher the idea for the title of this book—the fact that whenever they met while he was working for her, she was always asking him to find her a new way to die. In her first recorded song, 'L'étranger', the hapless marine ends up being fished out of the harbour after a night of passionate love. Subsequent Piaf 'demises' included dying of thirst in the desert ('Mon legionnaire'), being shot dead in a lift ('Le chasseur de l'hotel'), suicide (most famously in 'Les amants d'un jour'), execution by hanging ('Qu'as-tu fait John?'), and the bride's corpse being floated out to sea ('La chanson de Catherine'). Piaf also sang about child abuse ('Un monsieur me suit dans la rue'), and when two of her lovers—Félix Marten and Georges Moustaki—physically abused her, rather than go the authorities she punished them by getting a friend to write a song—'C'est un homme terrible'—detailing how they had used her for target practice. Better than anyone else, of course, she sang about love.

Piaf's taste in men befitted her complicated, anxious lifestyle. Invariably her lovers and husbands were mean and moody, or bisexual—or both. As Serge Reggiani reveals, when Piaf fell for Yves Montand he was involved with another man—who he promptly returned to once their ardour cooled, before he finally married Simone Signoret. Jacques Pills, as revealed by several interviewees, was a bisexual opportunist and by accounts not at all nice to know. Piaf's second husband, Théo Sarapo, was working as a male escort when they met—when he moved in with her, so did his boyfriend. Piaf even commissioned a song, 'Monsieur Incognito', which tells of his working his beat outside a Métro station in Paris. And yet the love they shared was heartfelt and genuine. Théo married Piaf aware that she had little time to live, and also aware that she was deeply in debt. French law dictated that he would have to settle these debts, when the time came.

Perhaps the most startling revelation of all is that Piaf had a second child, evidence of which exists not just in the photograph included here, but in the files at the Hôpital Tenon, in Paris, where Piaf's daughter Marcelle had been born. Indeed, Piaf herself was born here, and not as she liked to tell everyone, on a policeman's cape in front of the steps of 72 rue de Belleville—the building which contained her parents' tawdry room, in the early hours of 19 December 1915. Even so, her account is sufficiently amusing to fit in with the subsequent legends which abounded throughout her tragically short life, some real, mostly figments of an overworked imagination.

Piaf's father, Louis-Alphonse Gassion, worked as a street acrobat and contortionist, and was descended from a long line of circus entertainers. Measuring just 4'11", he was almost the same size as his daughter. Her mother, Line Marsa (Annette Maillard) was a half-Italian, half-Berber singer who, contrary to popular belief, did not just sing on street corners: as an exponent of rowdy *revencharde chansons* she had built up a modest following in the *beuglants* and *bal-musettes*. Marsa and Gassion had married in September 1914, but would spend virtually no time together after Piaf's birth. Marsa would later claim to have been carrying Gassion's child when they had separated, while their son, Herbert, would always claim only to be Piaf's *half*-brother. Given her character, he could have been fathered by anybody and there has never even been any evidence that Marsa was his mother, and that

Herbert, like the other siblings who turned up in the future, was just another opportunist. One must ask the question—had this been just an ordinary person and not one of the most famous women in France, would they have bothered?

The Gassion's daughter was baptized Édith, after the heroic English nurse, Édith Cavell, recently executed by the Germans. For a second name Marsa chose Giovanna, so that she would always be reminded of her Italian ancestry. Piaf hated the name, and the woman who had brought her into the world. In January 1916, Gassion returned to the Front, and Marsa dumped Édith with her mother, who lived in a filthy hovel on the rue Rebeval, not far from where she had been born. The child became ill, and when Gassion returned home in September 1917 he found her crawling with fleas and took her to live with his mother, who ran a brothel in Bernay, in Normandy. Here, she developed cataracts on her eyes and the doctor diagnosed conjunctivitis. Though we shall never know if she lost her sight completely, the 'miracle' of her restored vision that Piaf spoke about almost every day for the rest of her life had been effected by medicine, not as the result of a visit to Saint Thérèse's shrine at Lisieux. Thérèse Martin, the watchmaker's daughter from Alençon who had died, aged twenty-four, eighteen years before Piaf's birth, would not be canonized until May 1925. Even so, Piaf would always claim that her sight had returned on 21 August

1921, and for the rest of her life, Thérèse, with her shower of roses, would remain a key figure in her personal and religious development.

At around this time, Louis Gassion took Édith back to Paris, where she acted as his stooge in his pavement act. The mighty singing career began by chance in December 1926, when Gassion fell ill and was confined to his bed. With no money for food, and under threat of eviction from their landlord for non-payment of rent, Édith put on her overcoat and descended to the local square where she sang 'La Marseillaise', the only song she knew all the way through—earning as much for this as her father had made in three days. From now on, if Gassion was 'busy' with one of his many mistresses, Édith would go out on her own into the streets and sing. At the age of fifteen, having met Simone Berteaut—the infamous 'Mômone', or whom more later— she left Gassion for good, to make her own way in the world.

With Mômone as *her* stooge, Édith began singing in the streets on a regular basis. They earned a lot of money, and spent it recklessly without thinking where the next meal would be coming from. They slept rough, in rat-infested cellars and disused buildings, and were not choosy about the company they kept. Mômone's mother was no better than Line Marsa had been. While her daughter was paying her a weekly allowance from the salary she earned 'working for' Édith she did not create much of a fuss over the fact that both girls were breaking the law because they were minors. And then, Édith fell in love for the first time …

1. Louis Dupont

■　　■　　■

Louis Dupont (1913-1980) was Édith Gassion's first serious lover, whom she nicknamed 'P'tit Louis', not because he was small, but because he was over 6" tall—inasmuch as Little John in the Robin Hood legend was so named because of his great size. I met him in Paris in 1975, and was surprised that he had never been interviewed about Piaf before.

> We met on 21 March 1932 in Romainville, just outside Paris. Some years later, I'm sure by which time she'd forgotten all about me, she got two friends to write a song about it …

This was 'Y a pas de printemps', by Henri Contet and Marguerite Monnot, and which Piaf recorded in July 1944, long after Louis Dupont had exited her life:

> *Mais le destin m'a fait une farce,*
> *Le vingt et un du mois de mars.*
> *Quand le printemps chante à pleine voix sa naissance,*
> *Avec un beau gars m'a fait faire connaissance …*

[But destiny played a farce on me,
On the twenty-first of March.
When springtime was singing its birth in full voice
It acquainted me with a handsome boy …]

Why I first stumbled on this scruffy little kid, she was singing her heart out on a street corner. The song was Damia's 'J'ai le cafard', a rather depressing piece for one so young, and she really did look as though she had just stepped out of a dustbin. For weeks afterwards I kept asking myself what she'd had to make me fall head-over-heels in love with her. I guess it must have been her personality, or her cheek … And as for her temper—let me tell you, when Édith got out of bed the wrong side on a morning, *everyone* darted for cover.

Édith and P'tit Louis rented a room in the inaptly-named Hôtel de l'Avenir, in Belleville—Mômone moved in with them, mindless of the fact that the room only possessed one bed. A few months later, Édith fell pregnant, and P'tit Louis put his foot down—one of the rare occasions that Piaf allowed the man in her life to tell her what to do— declaring that singing in the streets while expecting a child amounted to little more than common vagrancy. For a few weeks she worked in a clogs factory, until her condition became obvious and she was fired. Her daughter, Marcelle, was born on 11 January 1933. Not long afterwards, Édith and Mômone returned to singing in the streets, taking the baby with them. P'tit Louis exacted his revenge by taking Marcelle away from her, declaring her an unfit mother.

By the Spring of 1935, Édith had progressed and was *chanteuse-en-résidence* at one of the most notorious gay bars in Paris, the Juan-les-Pins, in the heart of Pigalle's red-light district where, thieves, drug-addicts, and thugs mixed freely with respectable artistes such as Maurice Chevalier and Mistinguett. She was working here when P'tit Louis turned up one evening to inform her that their daughter had been taken to the hospital, where doctors had diagnosed spinal-meningitis. A week later, Marcelle Dupont died—an event which affected Piaf profoundly for the rest of her life. Since she had no money to pay for her daughter's funeral, the staff and clientele at the Juan-les-Pins had a whip-round, but she was still ten francs short. In desperation, she went out on the beat and picked up a man who took her to his hotel room, where instead of having sex with her, he gave her the money she needed, and left. In her second, more candid volume of memoirs she observed:

> In my career I've earned millions of francs, and I've
> squandered it all away because being a spendthrift
> was such fun. It was my revenge on myself for having
> slept on the pavement as a child. I have conquered

my own destiny which caused me to be born at
the bottom of the social scale, in the gutter where
hope hardly exists at all. But even the greatest of
my triumphs would never compensate for the most
atrocious memory of them all, the night when I was
so poor that I wanted to sell myself for ten francs.

Marcelle Dupont's death put paid to any future Piaf might
have been looking forward to with P'tit Louis, though they
remained friends for several years until he married and left
Paris, returning only for her funeral. By the time Louis
exited her life she was mixing with very rough company
indeed, and amorously involved with a trio of thugs: Albert,
a psychopathic legionnaire who beat her black-and-blue
and once pulled a gun on her and fired, the bullet missing
and grazing her neck; Léon, a regular at the Juan-les-Pins;
and a young sailor named Pierre. Louis Dupont could not
remember the first two, but he had known Pierre well:

> Everyone called him Le Balafré [Slasher] because
> he walked around with a cut-throat razor in his
> pocket. He was very good-looking, almost like a
> girl, and he would sleep with absolutely anyone,
> any age or either sex, so long as they could afford
> the going-rate, which was very high. Édith of
> course always charmed him into giving it to her for
> free—or should I say in exchange for the protection
> commission he charged on her earnings. Le Belafré's

hang-out was Gerny's, an expensive cabaret near l'Étoile. He was knocking off the owner, Louis Leplée.

Leplée (1875-1936) ran Gerny's, on rue Pierre-Charron, off the Champs-Elysées. He had discovered Édith singing on a nearby street-corner on 23 September 1935—performing another Damia song. It was Leplée who baptized her La Môme Piaf—*piaf* being the French slang word for *sparrow*. Like everyone she encountered at this time, he was a man with a shady reputation:

> For years, he'd made a living as a drag-artiste, working the halls until managing Chez Liberty—in the Twenties home to the most notorious perverts in Paris. He was never interested in any man older than twenty-five, and of course he had the money, not always honestly gained, to pay whatever they asked. Leplée ran a crime-ring which peddled drugs and underaged prostitutes, and Gerny's was merely a cover. Neither was the meeting between himself and Piaf an accident. It was engineered by Le Balafré, so that Le Balafré could screw her for even more money. Contrary to popular belief, she was no longer that unknown street-singer. Though she had never done more than four or five songs in any one performance, she was popular with the Pigalle crowd and had developed quite a following in that

part of town. She didn't have to sing in the streets anymore, but she did so because for her the smell of the traffic was like a drug ... Édith couldn't stand to be cooped up. Even when she was the biggest star in France she would occasionally put on old clothes and go out there for the sheer hell of it.

At Gerny's, where she opened on 26 September, just three days after Leplée discovered her, La Môme Piaf's repertoire did little to help her reputation. Her first song each evening was Vincent Scotto's 'Les mômes de la cloche', which told of the prostitutes who worked for a pittance in the most deprived suburbs of the city:

> C'est nous les mômes, les mômes de la cloche,
> Clochards qui s'en vont sans un rond en poche!
> C'est nous les paumées, les purées d'paumées,
> Qui sommes aimées un soir, n'importe où!

> [We're the kids, the guttersnipes,
> Tramps who roam around broke!
> We're the outcasts, the clapped-out outcasts,
> Who are loved for one night, no matter where!]

Anyone who was anyone in Paris went there to see her, some out of genuine admiration, others out of curiosity, the cynics amongst them believing that once Leplée's crimes caught up with him and he ended up in jail, his protégée would soon be back on the streets. Édith did herself few favours by accepting an invitation to sing at a dinner-party hosted by the cabinet minister, Jean de Rovera—his objective being that she would provide his guests with something to laugh at. Édith did not disappoint, drinking from the finger-bowl. The association with Leplée *did* end badly when, on 6 April 1936, he was found shot dead in his apartment.

Curiously, the interviewing of the chief witnesses and suspects was filmed and shown on cinema newsreels all over France, the featured attraction La Môme Piaf being bullied by Commissaire Guillaume, the officer in charge of the investigation. A Parisian tabloid even ran a *Bande-dessinée* (strip-cartoon). She was not suspected of firing the actual fatal shot, though the police *did* suspect that she may have been aware of the killer's identity—a lover she had shared with Leplée, as P'tit Louis explained:

> The killer was Le Belafré, of this there was absolutely no doubt. I'm equally certain, though, that Édith never knew this. She was so incredibly naïve— throughout her whole life, she only ever believed that the man of the moment had eyes for her. She even tried to get back with me, after Leplée's death. For me, however, enough was enough. Not long afterwards, having found the woman I hoped I might be sharing my life with, I left Paris and didn't return for many years.

2: Fernand Lumbroso

■   ■   ■

Six months after Louis Leplée's death, Piaf's career would be handled by Raymond Asso—then best-known for his collaborations with Marguerite Monnot for Piaf's favourite singer, the *fantaisiste* Marie Dubas. In the meantime, she found herself battered from pillar to post as she fought to cling to what very little reputation she had left. Bruno Coquatrix, who later ran the Olympia and became a close friend of Piaf, (and in many ways her saviour as will be seen) was then the director of Chez Odette, a gay club in Pigalle even seedier than the Juan-les-Pins. It was here that she wore a black dress for the first time, rather than the skirt and pullover she had worn at Gerny's. The engagement was a disaster—the clientele were interested only in the 'urchin' at the centre of the Leplée scandal. Coquatrix had offered her an open-ended contract, but she stayed less than a week before embarking on a tour of the local cinemas. And it was at this shaky stage of her career that she was reluctantly taken on by Fernand Lumbroso, the manager of the avant-garde *diseuse* Marianne Oswald. I got to know Fernand in 1990—a sprightly octogenarian, still 'up to tricks' as he put it, directing the Mogador in Paris, and presenting a new season of recitals by my friend, Barbara:

> Piaf was by far the most important thing that ever happened to me, now that I look back. But what a pain in the arse. I engaged her to play the cinemas between features. The first stop was Troyes, where she turned up with two men—a young thug who she said had told her he loved her almost as much as he loved his flick-knife, and an accordionist called Juel who would take any man apart as soon as look at him. Troyes wasn't too bad, but the real problems began in Brest, where a newspaper had announced the arrival of the next Yvonne George ...

Born in Belgium, Yvonne George (1896-1930) remains the most neurotic singer to have appeared on a French stage. Her biggest hit—adopted by the French Navy as their anthem—was 'Nous irons a Valparaiso'. A friend of Cocteau—who later befriended Piaf—George was an alcoholic, addicted to opium and suffering from bulimia. Almost everywhere she performed, there were riots, particularly in the seaports where she could frequently be seen leaving the theatre with a sailor on each arm. In 1930, suffering from tuberculosis and having been told that she did not have long to live, she was found dead in a hotel room of a drugs overdose. She and Piaf shared one song, 'Les prisons de Nantes'. Fernand explained what happened when Piaf had arrived in Brest, accompanied by the ubiquitous Mômone, where they had begun emulating Yvonne George by befriending sailors:

> As you know, the sailors were absolutely crackers about Yvonne George, so they all piled into the cinema, looking for a brawl with anyone who might not like her, even though most of them had never heard of her. She came on, did the three or four songs expected of her, then made the mistake of telling them she would be back after the main feature. This was *Lucretia Borgia*, so as you can imagine they were not in a very responsive mood. Then, when everyone should have been going home, she came on and announced that she was going to sing a song popularized by Marianne Oswald. She had sung 'Embrasse-moi' many times before, but this time she gave them 'En m'en foutant' [While Fucking Myself]. There was an all-out brawl and the cinema had to be evacuated. I got in touch with her and told her to *never* to sing that song again. The next night she sang 'Les hiboux', a self-mocking and extremely vulgar song about prostitution. The sailors started scrapping again, so the next morning I summoned her back to Paris. She frightened the life out of me when she barged into my office. Luckily, André Mauprey [Oswald's songwriter, and the man who had adapted Kurt

Weill's *The Threepenny Opera* into French] was with me at the time, and he took a shine to her ... He was over thirty years her senior, and within a week he'd taken her to bed. Inside another he'd written her a decent song ['Entre Saint-Ouen et Clignancourt'] about prostitution, if there was such a thing. Not long after that she ended up with Asso.

Some years later, in her memoirs, Piaf recalled this most distressing period of her life, and of how she had been rescued by her 'Cyrano', so nicknamed by her because of his sleeked back hair and large nose:

I had hit rock-bottom. So I rang him and confessed, 'I'm lost, Raymond, and I'm afraid that I'll do something stupid.' He told me to take a taxi, and I left for his place with nothing, not even a suitcase. I had shamed myself by wallowing in stupidity and ugliness, making a mess of the good things in life. Raymond taught me how to become a human being again, though it took him three years to disintoxicate me of Pigalle and my miserable, corrupted childhood.

3: Sylvie Galthier

Sylvie Galthier was the *frangine* (soul-sister-best-friend) of France's greatest ever *fantaisiste*, Marie Dubas (1894-1972), probably best described as France's answer to Gracie Fields in that she could switch from intense drama ('La Charlotte Prie Notre Dame') to buffoonery ('Butterfly-Tox') within the space of a song. For many years after Marie's death, until her own, Sylvie lived with Marie's only son, François Bellair, at their apartment just off the Etoile, in Paris. Warm and caring, sympathetic and sincere, it became apparent after our first meeting why Marie had called this extraordinary woman her 'rock'.

When Raymond Asso (1901-68) took Piaf under his wing, he must have known that he was onto a good thing—that even though raw around the edges, with the right person handling her, she would make it to the top. Therefore she was worth making any sacrifice for. Just as she had baptized him with an unflattering moniker, he called her his 'Spanish beggar', which was probably apt at the time. When he became her mentor he was living with Madeleine, his common-law wife, and Piaf was still encumbered with

Mômone. As with Louis Dupont, it was love at first sight, and Asso was ordered to get rid of Madeleine, 'or else'. He promptly did so, and in the not too distant future, he would also drop Marie Dubas, for whom he was working at the time. Sylvie explained:

> Piaf did not have a good reputation in those days. She was accused of stealing songs from other singers, but she had no choice because she had no songwriters of her own. Marie didn't mind this—in her opinion everyone had to start somewhere. They first met in October 1935 at the Empire, courtesy of Raymond Asso, who was then working as Marie's secretary and dabbling at songwriting. Marie hated making records and made comparatively few despite her vast repertoire, but she had a recording machine which she used to monitor audience reaction to certain songs. Piaf was working at Gerny's at the time, and audaciously asked Marie if she might sing something into this machine.

The song was 'La java en mineur', written by Asso for Marie Dubas, and in a Parisian vernacular which even many French listeners might not have understood. The machine appears to have been one which produced acetates. Piaf recorded the song on 15 October, and as such it preceded the better-known 'L'étranger' and 'Les mômes de la cloche', which she recorded in the studio on 18 December, the eve of her twentieth birthday. With Asso accompanying her on the piano, Piaf occasionally breaks off from singing to yell instructions at the stagehand working the machine. The recording was subsequently transferred to a tape and played for the first time on France-Inter radio in June 1981, though Piaf never sang it on the stage. Many years later, she wrote in her memoirs:

> Marie Dubas was my inspiration, my joy and my sadness. She alone created the *chanson* as we know it today, with its three verses and refrains. She knew how to make the public laugh, whereas I only know how to make them cry. Marie is the greatest star there has ever been. I owe everything to her.

Asso was impressed with Piaf's singing, and a few weeks later presented her with 'Mon légionnaire'— which he had written especially for her, having heard that she had cheated on Louis Dupont with a légionnaire, who had been transferred to North Africa, where he had subsequently died:

> *Il était plein de tatouages,*
> *Son cou portait: 'Pas vu, pas pris',*
> *Sur son coeur on lisait, 'Personne',*
> *Sur son bras droit un mot, 'Raisonne'.*
> *J'sais pas son nom, je n'sais rien de lui,*
> *Il m'a aimée toute la nuit, mon légionnaire …*

[He was covered in tattoos,
On his neck: 'Neither seen nor taken',
Across his heart, 'Nobody',
On his right arm one word, 'Truth'.
I don't know his name, I know nothing about him,
He loved me all night long, my légionnaire …]

In this song, the légionnaire is found in the desert, his lifeless eyes staring up at the sun. The story turned out to be fabrication. In her memoirs Piaf recounts how, many years later, he turned up at one of her recitals—fat and balding. For now, Piaf accused Asso of 'taking the piss', and told him in no uncertain terms what to do with his song. He promptly gave it to Marie Dubas, who recorded it in May, a few weeks after the Leplée murder—with Asso's 'Le fanion de la Légion' on the flipside:

Ah! La-la-la-la belle histoire!
Ils restent trois dans le bastion,
Le torse nu, couverts de gloire.
Sanglants, meurtris et en haillons,
Sans eau, ni pain, ni munitions,
On leur a volé le fanion,
Le beau fanion de la Légion!

[Ah, what a fine story!
There are three left in the bastion,
Bare-chested, clothed in glory.

Bloodstained, battered and in rags,
With neither water, bread nor munitions,
They've stolen the flag!
The beautiful flag of the Légion!]

Piaf, in the meantime, had arrived back in Paris after the tour organized by Fernand Lumbroso. To 'punish' Asso she took up with a young poet named Roméo Carlés. Their affair lasted long enough for him to write two songs—'Simple comme bonjour' and 'La petite boutique'. Because of the Leplée affair, no theatre would hire her—and when Carlés refused to write her more songs, declaring that he was not a machine, she went back to Asso, who secured her future by agreeing to manage her. He left Marie Dubas' employ, and he and Piaf moved into the Hôtel Alsina, in Montmartre, where they embarked on a tempestuous relationship which produced some of Piaf's most stunning songs. Sylvie recalled:

> Marie was at the ABC. The Leplée murder was still in the newspapers, and I was surprised that Marie agreed to see her. Piaf was very rough around the edges, and could fight like any man. She had a black eye, but Asso had two. This time when she saw Marie she actually knelt at her feet and kissed her hand. Piaf told Marie that 'Mon légionnaire' had made her cry, and added that Asso had originally written it for her. Marie had not known

this, and she felt guilty. Then Piaf sang a verse from the song, and this made Marie cry. Marie was delighted when Piaf recorded both of the Légion songs, early the following year. Many years later, they shared another song, 'Monsieur est parti en voyage'. More importantly, they shared a close friendship—and a profound mutual respect—which lasted until Piaf died.

It was through Asso's persistent hounding that Piaf was given top-billing at the ABC, then the most prestigious music-hall in Paris, and one renowned for paying stingy fees. She opened here on 26 March 1937—no longer as La Môme Piaf, the name linked to the Leplée scandal, but Édith Piaf. In an exclusive programme of Asso songs she was an absolute triumph. The music for all of these was by Marguerite Monnot, who very quickly became her closest friend—soon she would be collaborating with 'Guite', as she nicknamed her, and for years they would be the most successful female songwriting partnership in Europe. For Piaf, one hit followed another, though she always maintained that her proudest moment was when she shared top-billing at the ABC with Marie Dubas:

> I was with Marie when Marie asked her, 'Édith, why do you always address me as *vous*, instead of *tu*? I look upon you almost as a younger sister.' And Piaf replied, with tears in her eyes, 'If I did that, the *magic* would disappear!' And she was like that every

time she met Marie, like the fans are with Johnny Hallyday, giddy and breathless and absolutely awestruck.

The relationship with Asso became even more tempestuous as Édith's star ascended. He was not averse to employing his fists to silence her whenever she went off on one of her foul-mouthed rants—and she was not averse to hitting him back with whatever came to hand. During one particularly violent confrontation in the early spring of 1938, she walked out on him and took up once more with Roméo Carlés, and it was almost certainly he who got her pregnant—one aspect of Édith's life which I did not feel obliged to reveal while Sylvie Galthier was alive, for it was she who revealed the exclusive:

> In September 1938, Marie was singing in Nice when Édith turned up unexpectedly. It was a warm day, yet she was wearing an overcoat, and this was buttoned right up to her throat. When she removed this in Marie's room, she had quite a bump. Marie asked if the child was Asso's, and Édith said not. The child could of course have been anybody's, in those days, but she was convinced that Roméo Carlés was the father. She made Marie and myself swear never to tell a living soul about her condition, though I'm sure everyone who worked with her at the time must have known, most especially Asso.

Édith returned to Paris on 30 September, and on 3 October spent the afternoon in the studio where she recorded four songs, all by Asso, including 'C'est lui que mon coeur a choisi'. Her condition now made it impossible for her to appear on stage, and for several weeks she almost became a recluse. On 12 November, she recorded a second version of 'Mon légionnaire'—this one has a fine violin solo from Stephane Grapelli, though he is not credited on the label. The next morning, she collapsed and—ironically perhaps— she was taken to the Hôpital Tenon, where doctors told her that for the past week she had been carrying a dead baby, the result of umbilical cord strangulation. On 14 November, she was delivered of a son, and at the time surgeons carried out a hysterectomy. Sylvie explained:

> Marie visited her in the hospital. She was weak, but seemed cheerful—though Marie was convinced that she was only putting on a brave front, knowing that she would never be able to have children. Had all of this happened today [in 1988], something might have been done to save the child. Back then, I'm sure that all that mattered to her was keeping the story out of the papers while the Leplée scandal was still being talked about.

4: Michel Émer

■　　　■　　　■

Between January 1937 and the summer of 1939, virtually everything Piaf sang had been written by Raymond Asso—one song, 'Je n'en connais pas la fin', would later be adapted into English as 'My Lost Melody' and serve as her theme song in America. She stayed with him until August 1939, when he was called up. This set a precedent as to how to treat the men in her life, who invariably used *her* for what he could get out of her, once the flames of passion had started to cool. She found a replacement before he was even gone, though not one who could help her with her singing career.

The new man was Paul Meurisse (1912-79), a singer friend of Marie Dubas working the nightclub circuit—as snobbish and sophisticated as Piaf was down to earth and uncultured. Within days, Meurisse moved into Piaf's room at the Alsina, staying there only long enough for the woman he had been living with to vacate his apartment on the rue Anatole-la-Forge, near l'Étoile. The couple then moved there, and from this point their relationship plummeted to the depths of neurosis—with Meurisse lounging around all day in his dressing-gown, reading his newspaper and trying to ignore Piaf's nagging and yelling. When she related this to her newest friend, Jean Cocteau, he wrote them a one-act play, *Le bel indifférent*. This opened at the Bouffes-Parisiens in the Spring of 1940, and was an unprecedented triumph.

The affair with Meurisse lasted for the few months that *Le bel indifférent* played to packed houses, and until Piaf had made her first major film, with him as one of the co-stars. He would give up his singing career and go on to become one of France's best-loved and most versatile actors. His most famous role would be that of the sadistic headmaster in *Les diabloliques* (1955).

There was also Michel Émer (1906-84), who Piaf initially made fun of because he was thin and wore bottle-bottom spectacles. They met in the spring of 1940 and their relationship lasted until the end of her career. They were never lovers, which was why he lasted the course whilst others dropped by the wayside. Émer told me about his extraordinary stroke of luck, *chez* Piaf:

> Édith was preparing for a new season at the Bobino, and I must have caught her in a bad mood. When her secretary announced that there was a young man at the door with a song she might be interested in, I heard her yell, 'Any excuse. Tell him to fuck off and come back after the war!' So I shouted back, 'And if I'm killed, madame, you'll have missed out

on one of the best songs you never had the patience to listen to!' At this she came to the door, took one look at me and barked, 'Bugger me, it's Tojo. You'd better come in.' Then she added insult to injury by pointing to my corporal's uniform and saying, 'Until now I've never been able to resist a man in uniform, but it looks like even I'm going to have to draw a line somewhere. Tell me about yourself— you've got five minutes.' There was little to tell: I was in my early thirties, from a respectable Jewish family, and I was stationed at Val-de-Grâce, off boulevard Port-Royal. I'd also been given explicit instructions to return there by midnight—or run the risk of court marshal ... So I sat at the piano and sang 'L'accordéoniste'. All the way through, Piaf had her fingers in her ears and I was sure she was displeased with the song. Later she said it had been my voice—I've always been tone-deaf. She asked me to play the song again, this time *without* singing it. When I'd finished she threw her hands in the air and cried, 'Formidable! I'll sing it at the Bobino premiere!' I was horrified, for the premiere was only twenty-four hours off, and I was worried about getting back to base. Then she told her secretary to get my commanding officer on the line. God knows what she said to him, but I stayed with her until five the next morning, going over the song more than a hundred times. And there was no court marshal.

'L'accordéoniste' was the first Piaf recording to sell over a million copies. It is the classic *chanson-réaliste*, telling of the prostitute who falls for the accordionist at her local dance-hall. And though all does not go according to plan, the couple can at least still aspire to the future:

> *La fille de joie est triste, au coin d'la rue là-bas,*
> *Son accordéoniste il est parti soldat.*
> *Quand il r'viendra d'la guerre,*
> *Ils prendront une maison,*
> *Elle sera la caissière et lui sera l'patron ...*

> [The prostitute is sad, on the street corner over there,
> Her accordionist has gone off to be a soldier.
> When he returns from the war,
> They'll take over a 'house',
> She'll be cashier and he'll be the boss ...]

The man does not return from the war, and in desperation the girl goes back on the beat, only to find that another accordionist occupies the same spot as her dead lover. Finally, unable to stand anymore, she screams for the music to stop. 'L'accordéoniste' would give Piaf one of her biggest hits. Even in America, at a time when such lascivious subject matter was frowned upon, it was one of her most requested songs. Piaf also boasted that Michel Émer was twice as talented as most of her other regular songwriters, in that he wrote both words *and* music for her songs. She was also more ruthless to him than she was to some of the others:

> I remember the first time I went to America with her. I was looking forward to having a night on the town with the rest of the gang and seeing the sights of New York—but she confined me to me room, locking the door from the outside, saying that she would only let me out after I'd written her a song. I did better than that and wrote two. 'Bal dans ma rue' is about a woman who introduces her lover to her best friend—who subsequently runs off with him. And 'Monsieur Lenoble' told of the man who takes everyone for granted, most especially his wife who leaves him for a younger man. Piaf was always looking for a new way to die, and in this one he gasses himself. The Americans used to howl with laughter when she imitated the hissing of the gas-taps.

Monsieur Lenoble se mouche,
Met sa chemise de nuit,
Ouvre le gaz, et se couche.
Demain, tout sera fini ...

[Monsieur Lenoble blows his nose,
Puts on his nightshirt,
Turns on the gas and goes to bed,
Tomorrow it will all be over ...]

5: Damia

■　　■　　■

During World War II, Piaf became one of the unsung heroines of the Résistance. For many years, some biographers—though never the French ones—speculated whether Piaf might have collaborated with the Nazis, but nothing could have been further from the truth. Indeed, had there been the slightest suspicion of this, the Tricolor would not have been allowed to be draped over her coffin at her funeral, and she would not have been assigned a detachment from the French Foreign Legion. Similar investigations took place with Mistinguett, Joséphine Baker, Tino Rossi and Maurice Chevalier—with the latter two being refused any State honours because, though there was no actual proof that they had collaborated, there was no proof that they had not.

Like everybody else, she had to report regularly to the German *Propagandastaffel* on the Champs-Elysées to have the lyrics to her songs vetted. She was ticked off for singing the biting 'Il n'est pas distingué', which made fun of Hitler, but refused to remove the intensely patriotic 'Où sont-ils mes petits copains' from her repertoire. She fared well under the Germans, not because she kowtowed like many of her colleagues, but because she was unafraid of standing up to them, and in doing so earned their respect. Some of her Jewish friends were not so fortunate. Marcel Blistène (of whom more later) and Michel Émer fled to the South. Marie Dubas had her house seized by the Gestapo, and would spend the rest of the war in neutral Portugal. Piaf despised the Nazis, yet was pragmatically circumspect in her relations with the *Propagandastaffel* personnel in order to achieve her goal—singing for French prisoners at Stalag III, in Germany.

After each show at the camp, Piaf and her secretary, Andrée Bigard, were allowed to mingle with some of the prisoners. She had a phenomenal memory, and would remember their names and addresses—then she would ask the commandant if she could have her photograph taken with them and the officers, so that those back home could see how well they were being looked after. The ruse worked every time. The photographs were enlarged, and the head and shoulders shots mounted onto forged identity papers and sneaked back into the camp—Piaf never had trouble being asked back for a repeat performance. The prisoners were smuggled out a few at a time. The camp authorities trusted her so implicitly that they never realized she was arriving with an entourage of seventeen, and leaving with twenty-two. In all, she enabled some three hundred prisoners to escape to the Unoccupied Zone, and also chartered a ship to bring some of them from Marseilles to England. *This* was why the tricolour was draped over her coffin.

With Piaf and Paul Meurisse clinging to their affair by the slenderest of threads, and having seen them in *Le bel indifférent*, early in 1941 they were approached by the film director Georges Lacombe and shown the script for *Montmartre-sur-Seine*. Piaf had already made a brief appearance in a film, singing 'Quand même' in *La garçonne*, a Sapphic drama starring Suzy Solidor. She accepted the part without hesitation of the flower-seller from Montmartre who falls in love with a local boy who, ironically perhaps, is in love with someone else. He was played by Henri Vidal, one of the handsomest actors to have graced the Continental screen. Also in the film was the great actor, Jean-Louis Barrault, who was a friend of Damia (Marie-Louise Damien, 1889-1978) France's greatest female singer, pre-Piaf. There were other such *monstres-sacrés*, as the French called them— Fréhel, Lys Gauty and Suzy Solidor were but three—but none even remotely matched up to Damia's hyper-dramatic style and electrifying stage presence. She was the first artiste to perform dressed entirely in black—setting a trend since adapted by every *chanteuse-réaliste* worthy of mention— and with a spotlight directly trained on her face. Damia's career had begun on the eve of World War I, and she retired in 1956—ironically bowing out on *La joie de vivre de Gilbert Bécaud*, almost the French equivalent of Britain's *This Is Your Life*, singing 'Les croix', which Bécaud had written for Piaf. For a while, the two singers were fierce rivals, though they later became friends, as she recalled:

> In her early days, Piaf was a thief. She didn't have any songwriters of her own, so she stole ours. One of my big numbers in those days was 'Les deux ménétriers', the one she was supposed to be singing when Leplée discovered her. Piaf went around telling everyone it was *hers*, and as you imagine, that really stuck in my throat. She also stole material from Marie Dubas and Marianne Oswald, and began copying *my* style, until my agent went to see [Raymond] Asso and told him that this would have to stop. Then one evening I came offstage at the Concert-Pacra and she was waiting in my dressing-room with a huge bunch of flowers. After that she began respecting me, and we became rather good friends. She loaned me several of her songs, and even wrote one especially for me.

Two of the songs written for the film by Piaf and Marguerite Monnot were 'Un coin tout bleu' and 'Tu es partout'—years later, both of these appeared on the soundtrack of Steven Spielberg's blockbuster movie of 1998, *Saving Private Ryan*, introducing a new generation of American fans to the Piaf catalogue:

Je te vois partout dans le ciel,
Je te vois partout sur la terre,
Tu es ma joie et mon soleil,
Ma nuit, mes jours, mes aubes claires!

[I see you everywhere on heaven
I see you everywhere on earth,
You're my joy and my sunshine,
My night, my days, by bright dawns!]

One afternoon, Jean-Louis Barrault brought Damia to the set, and she was bowled over by what she heard:

Two of the songs ['J'ai dansé avec l'amour' and 'L'homme des bars'] were average, but the other two, 'Tu es partout' and 'Un coin tout bleu', were years ahead of their time. So, swallowing a huge piece of humble pie, I told her this ... And what do you think happened? This tiny slip of a thing with the vocabulary of a docker suddenly burst into tears and said, 'Madame, now they're *yours*.' She even accompanied me to the studio to supervise the session, and from that day, I completely changed my opinion of her. She even wrote one song especially for me. And so far as I know, she never sang that song herself. *[sings]*

Je ne veux pas rentrer chez moi,
Mon coeur a trop peur d'avoir froid.
Mon amour vient de finir,
Mon amour vient de partir.
Je n'ai plus aucun desire …
Mon amour vient de mourir!

[I don't want to go home,
My heart's too afraid to be cold.
My love has just ended,
My love has just gone away.
I have no more desire,
My love has just died!]

6: Manouche

■　　　■　　　■

The next man in Piaf's life was Henri Contet (1904-98). When they met he was doubling as the director Georges Lacombe's press-attaché whilst reporting for *Cinémonde* and *France-Soir*. Tall and blond, Piaf fell for him when she learned that he also wrote songs as a sideline. He is also thought to have been the only Piaf lyricist who never worked with her composers, preferring to hand them to her, and let her decide who should set them to music. Contet would supply her with some of her finest songs, including 'Padam, padam', 'Les amants de demain', and the sublime 'Les neiges de Finlande'. His first, presented to her in November 1942, was 'La demoiselle du cinquième', which she never recorded:

> *La demoiselle, qui avait tant de peine,*
> *C'était à prévoir, voulut se tuer.*
> *Elle a voulu se jeter dans la Seine,*
> *Voulu ... ou du moins elle en a parlé!*

> [The lady, who had so much pain,
> Predictably, tried to kill himself.

She wanted to throw himself into the Seine,
Wanted to … or at least she has talked about it!]

The fact that Contet was as good as married mattered little
to Piaf, and after completing *Montmartre-sur-Seine*, having
given Paul Meurisse his marching orders, she moved into a
new apartment—a few doors from the one she had shared
with Meurisse, and asked Contet to move in with her.
Initially, he refused, so she tried to make him jealous by
flirting with Yvon Jean-Claude, a young singer who was just
breaking into the Parisian cabaret scene. Earlier in the year,
Piaf had recorded a duet, 'Le vagabond', with Jean-Claude,
and she now really rubbed salt into Contet's wounds by
putting 'Cétait une histoire d'amour' into her repertoire—
and having Jean-Claude walk on to the stage, wrap his arms
around her, and join in with the final refrain.

The ruse worked, and Contet moved in with her—
though Yvon Jean-Claude, referred to by Piaf as 'my fuck
on demand', would not see his services as a stud dispensed
with for another two years. Then, when fuel rationing was
introduced, Piaf moved out of the apartment to rent the
entire third floor of Madame Billy's infamous bordello on
rue Villejuste (now rue Paul Valéry). Living here, she said,
would bring her luck because, like the brothel in Bernay,
it had two pianos. It was also a favourite haunt of German
officers—and by being seen to be friendly with these, Piaf

was offered an invaluable cover for her work with the Résistance. She stayed here for two years with her 'team'—Contet, Andrée Bigard, Mômone, and Tchang, her Chinese cook until the brothel was closed down on account of Billy's black market racketeering.

Since appearing in his play, Jean Cocteau had nicknamed Piaf 'La Coqueluche des Intellectuels'—'The Darling of the Intellectuals'—and as such, anyone who was anyone from the acting, literary and music-hall fraternity was welcome at her parties, which raged on all night at Billy's *maison-close*. She was also visited by her parents. Louis Gassion, retired now and in poor health, came to collect the food parcels Piaf had made up. For years she had been trying to get him to move away from Belleville, and had recently provided him with a manservant, which of course had made him the talk of the district—absolutely no one in this part of Paris could afford hired help. As for Line Marsa, she made a nuisance of herself by scrounging money for drink and drugs. She had served a prison sentence for trafficking, but the worst insult of all came when Michel Émer sent Piaf the sheet music for 'De l'autre côté de la rue', which he had written whilst in exile. Piaf's mother had rubbed salt into her wounds by performing the song in public:

> *Des murs qui se lézardent, un escalier étroit,*
> *Une vieille mansard, et me voilà chez moi.*

De l'autre côté de la rue y'a une fille, une belle fille,
Vivre un seul jour sa vie,
J'n'en demand'rais pas plus …

[Cracked walls, a narrow staircase,
An old attic room, that's my place!
On the other side of the street there's a beautiful girl,
I would ask for nothing more
Than to live one day of her life …]

While living at Madame Billy's, Piaf was befriended by Manouche (Germaine Germain), the copiously vulgar former mannequin and mistress of the Corsican gangster, Paul Carbone, a collaborator recently murdered by the Résistance. His story would be told in the 1970 film, *Borsalino*. Piaf rarely spoke about her mother—if her name came up in conversation, her comments were never less than scathing, as Manouche recalled:

> Piaf—I never once addressed her by her first name—offered me a strong shoulder to cry on, in those dark, horrible days. Whenever you were with her there was never a dull moment. A group of us were gathered in Billy's sitting room. The window was half-open and Piaf was singing Mistinguett's 'Mon homme' when all of a sudden this other voice came floating up from the street below—almost a copy of Piaf's voice, singing 'Mon légionnaire'. Piaf

screwed up her face and yelled at Cocteau, 'It's my fucking mother. Hurry up and pass me the piss-pot!' When I rushed to the window, I saw Line Marsa out in the street. She was dressed in red, rocking back and forth as if in pain. Cocteau ignored Piaf's instruction, and threw her a banknote. Line Marsa hoisted her skirts, pretended to wipe her backside on it, and left. Piaf slammed the window shut, and I think she assumed she'd seen the last of her. No such luck. Every morning for two weeks she was out there, crowing until one of us threw her some more money to shut her up. One day she brought this young man with her, spinning us some yarn that he was Gassion's and her kid, and Piaf's brother. When Piaf questioned this, Line Marsa said that she'd handed him over when he was a kid to be brought up by the Public Assistance. Piaf didn't believe one word of it, and a few days later she sent one of her heavies around to warn her to keep away. In fact, it turned out to be unnecessary ...

On 6 February 1945, Piaf's mother died of a drugs overdose, aged forty-nine. At the time she was living with a male prostitute half her age—Louis Gassion had divorced her in 1929. Terrified he might be busted by the police, her companion dragged her body out of their apartment and dumped it in the gutter. The previous year Piaf had given her father a magnificent send-off—he was buried in the vault at Père Lachaise, which she had bought for herself. Yvon Jean-Claude had helped her make all the arrangements. She refused to be involved with Line Marsa's funeral arrangements and did not even attend the ceremony. She did however allow her to be buried in Marcelle Dupont's grave on the outskirts of Paris—but only after her little daughter had been transferred to the vault in Père Lachaise.

Manouche was the god-daughter of Mistinguett [Jeanne Florentine Bourgeois], a frequent visitor to Billy's, and also secretly working with the Résistance. She referred to Piaf as 'that little thing in black', and never by name. Manouche spoke of the 'connection' between the seventy-five-year-old revue star and Piaf: the cyclist, Louis 'Toto' Gérardin (1912-82), who at the same time happened to be the lover of my godfather, Roger Normand. In November 1951, Toto left them both to move in with Piaf:

> Miss [Mistinguett] and Piaf were both totally unreasonable where men were concerned, making all sorts of impossible demands on their men. Both had an unfortunate knack of choosing men who were already spoken for, or the ones like Toto who licked both sides of the stamp. Miss didn't mind *who* her men were sleeping with so long as they crawled into her bed every now and then. Believe me, there was never any shortage of takers … Piaf, on the

other hand, was so insanely *jealous*. If Toto went
to the toilet on his own, she would start screaming
that he'd been having it off with somebody in the
bathroom. And despite his philandering he was
a gentle man, but also a very stupid one. Alice,
his wife, nagged him and knocked him around.
Miss pampered him and fussed around him like a
mother-hen. Piaf kept him on an invisible chain.
Most of the time the poor boy didn't know whether
he was coming or going. Is there any wonder he
made a mistake?

The 'mistake' was revealed in December 1951, when Alice
Gérardin hired a private detective to follow the couple.
When moving in with Piaf, Toto had taken most of the
family valuables with him—including eighteen gold ingots.
Piaf was arrested on suspicion of handling stolen goods and
interrogated—the police later confessed the interview was
just for the hell of it. The incident made the headlines:

> The flics had questioned more than a dozen of her
> friends, and we all said the same thing. Wherever
> she lived—and no matter how long she'd lived
> there—Piaf's place always looked as though she'd
> just moved in. Apart from the salon, every room
> was cluttered with boxes and packing cases. There
> was so much junk, half the time she didn't know
> *what* was hers. And all those freeloaders. Once a

guy stayed for two weeks, and when he left, none of us knew who he'd been. It turned out that he'd been a television repair-man, and every night his mates had come to the house and feasted like kings. Piaf wouldn't have had anything in the house that was hot. That's why she flushed a million francs' worth of jewels Toto had given her down the toilet, once she'd kicked him out into the street.

Gérardin returned to his wife, and later remarked of his adventure, 'Forty-eight hours with Piaf are more tiring than a lap of the Tour de France.' Piaf, meanwhile, made an attempt to rid herself of 'Toto's stink' by hiring one of the costliest interior designers in Paris to modernize her apartment—only to realize as soon as it was finished what a mistake this had been:

> She spent money she couldn't afford having the place done over by one of the most expensive interior designers in France, but as soon as she saw the blue satin bedroom, she was terrified of stepping inside it in case she dirtied it. And when she saw the rose-mosaic sunken bath, she filled it with goldfish.

7: Serge Reggiani

■　　　■　　　■

Serge Reggiani (1922-2004) will be remembered as one of the finest singers of his generation, and one of the best-loved. Singing, however, was not his first chosen vocation. Born in Reggio Emilia, Italy, he moved to Paris with his parents in 1930. During the war, while starting out on his career as a stage actor he was a key figure with the Résistance. Then, with peacetime, the opportunity had come for him to appear in his first film:

> Yves Montand was one of my best friends at that time [1945]. We were both Italians, though we'd spent most of our lives living in France, and we were just starting out in our acting careers. Piaf had met Yves by way of her agent. He always said that she was in some ways the best thing that had ever happened to her, and in other ways his very worst nightmare.

Piaf had been singing professionally for ten years, but still had no agent. Intermittently she had been handled by the OSA, the agency which managed the singer Lucienne Delyle, who she would never like, and Michel Émer.

In April 1944, Louis Barrier—a man with absolutely no business experience—entered her life. She was walking through the street one day when he almost knocked her down with his bicycle and, recognizing her and by way of an apology … he asked her if he could be her manager. Piaf was so bowled over by his nerve that she agreed. She would never stay with the same man for very long, but 'Loulou', as she baptized him, would handle her affairs until the day she died. Within a week of becoming her 'right-hand' man, he had secured her a two-week stint at the Moulin Rouge, then a temple for the *chanson* and not the tourist-trap of the present day. He also persuaded the management to allow Piaf to choose the *vedette-américaine*, in France the artiste secondary to the top of the bill, and who closes the first half of the show. She chose Yves Montand (1921-91), a crooner who would set another precedent as the first in a long line of artistes she would alternatively love, nurture, mould and bully towards national and international fame.

Born Yvo Livi in Monsumato Alto, he had moved with his family to Marseilles to escape the fascism of Mussolini. After leaving school he had worked as a docker before trying his hand as a singer—performing cowboy songs, and the works of his idol, Charles Trenet. Piaf had seen him at the ABC when he had supported André Dassary. She later wrote in her memoirs:

I didn't understand what people saw in him. He sang badly, couldn't dance and had no timing. But once I allowed myself to be pushed into taking him on, I realized at once that I would make something of him. The young are always the same when starting out ... They think the world is going to be bowled over by their cynicism and wit. So I told him, 'Nobody's going to be bowled over by *you*.'

As Serge Reggiani said, Piaf really did put Montand through the mill. She, whose own great quality was that she never lost her own Bellevilloise *argot*, denounced his Marseille accent and in order to rid him of it, made him sing for hours with a pencil between his teeth. She made him stop wearing his loud-check 'country and western' jackets and sing in his shirt-sleeves, thus highlighting his superb silhouette—second only to Piaf's, until Barbara took Paris by storm in the early Sixties.

The first stumbling block was Montand's lover, the singer Reda Caire, who had begun his career partnering Mistinguett. Piaf always believed that Montand had sent him packing, but like her 'stud', Yvon Jean-Claude, he would always be lingering in the background. She then ordered him to stop singing the mock cowboy songs written for him by the blind composer, Charles Hummel. With the Liberation just around the corner, she declared, his fake Americanisms would make him the butt of everyone's jokes once the real Americans arrived on the scene. With incredible nerve, she asked Henri Contet to write him a complete repertoire of new songs—not a wise thing to do considering she was only stringing Contet along until she had made Montand fall for her, the way she had fallen for him. Serge recalled:

> That was Piaf. She never let one man go until she'd found a replacement, so to make Yves fall in love with her, she convinced him that she would also make an actor out of him, as she had Paul Meurisse. Marcel Blistène was making *Étoile sans lumière* and had hired her to play the lead, therefore she insisted that Yves be hired to play the part of her leading man. He agreed, then Yves asked Blistène if I could have a part—it was easier in those days. There were no screen tests. If the director thought you were good enough, you got the part. Piaf never let Yves out of her sight for a moment, well aware that Blistène fancied him. For a little while she fixed her sights on me. She always thought ahead— you know, as soon as there were cracks in the relationship, to start looking for a replacement. She and Yves were already having problems. I wasn't interested in her, not in *that* way, besides which I had nothing to offer her. I wasn't a singer [then], and I wasn't writing songs. I have to confess that

for a novice she was a tremendous actress ... It's sad that she appeared in so few films. She could easily have become the French equivalent of Anna Magnani. *Étoile sans lumière* was a good film, but only because she was in it. It contained too many mistakes.

The 'mistakes'—picked up on by the critics—had much to do with the action taking place in 1929, while the clothes, hairstyles, cars, telephones and studio equipment were all from 1945. Despite this the film was a massive success, even in America, which was unusual for a subtitled film. *Étoile sans lumière* would later be remade as *Singin' in the Rain*, with Gene Kelly and Debbie Reynolds. It tells the story of Stella Dora (Mila Parély), a celebrated star from the silent era who is desperate to make the transition to the newly-arrived talkies, save that she has failed her voice-test. She and her team therefore attempt to keep her in the spotlight by duplicitous means. Stella's agent hears his maid, Madeleine (Piaf) singing as she goes about her chores, and decides to take advantage of her. He gets his technician (Reggiani) to record her voice, telling her that she has what it takes to become a famous singer. What she does not know is that her voice will be dubbed over Stella's in a film. When she finally learns the truth during the film's premiere—Stella mimes to the superb 'Adieu mon coeur' whilst her character is chained to the wall in her prison cell—she is upset, and the agent tries to make amends by offering her an engagement in a music hall. In rehearsal—in a sequence filmed on stage in the empty ABC—she sings 'Mariage', pulling out all the stops. Piaf would often close her American recitals with this one, bringing a titter from audiences when announcing, 'A woman has just been arrested for killing her husband … '

> *Car tout était miraculeux,*
> *L'église chantait rien que pour eux!*
> *Et même le pauvre était heureux !*
> *Et là-haut à toute volée,*
> *Les cloches criaient, 'Vive la mariée!'*

> [It was miraculous,
> The church singing for them alone!
> And even the poor man was happy!
> And high above, in full peal,
> The bells were screaming, 'Long live the bride!']

The show itself does not go well. Madeleine's first song is 'C'est merveilleux', the one she has earlier sung to her lover, Pierre (Montand) in the film's most famous sequence, while they are driving through the country just before their car breaks down. Attempting to sing this in front of an audience, she dries up. Stella, filled with remorse, commits suicide—whilst Madeleine returns to her village to be consoled by Pierre. Serge explained:

> Marcel Blistène made her sing that song over and over again, pretending that it had been a bad take. It hadn't—he just wanted to hear her beautiful singing. But there was also a great deal of tension on the set because the soundtrack had been written by Piaf's former lover, Henri Contet. He visited the set every day, and when Piaf saw how much this was annoying Yves, she started flirting with Contet. Yves exacted his revenge by spending the night with his old flame, Réda Caire—so far as I know, the only homosexual relationship he ever had. This didn't bother Piaf. She called Yvon Jean-Claude, a singer she had been involved with a few years earlier. They were in bed the next night at her hotel when Yves came banging on the door. Yvon was forced to hide in the wardrobe for hours, stark naked, until Piaf and Yves had finished making love and were asleep—then he escaped through the window. Life was so complicated in those days!

The Piaf-Montand relationship dragged on for a few months until shortly after the release of *Étoile sans lumière*—effectively, until she had fulfilled her latest mission as Svengali and moved on to her next 'Trilby', while Montand returned to Réda Caire, and a few years later met Simone

Signoret, who he married and who will always be regarded as the great love of his life.

Montand and Reggiani scarcely paused for breath before appearing together in *Les portes de la nuit*, hailed as one of the most celebrated French films of the Forties. Then, as Montand's career as an all-round entertainer moved from strength to strength, for Reggiani there was an abrupt change of direction—in 1965, and at the age of forty-three. Courtesy of Barbara, who engaged him as *vedette-américaine* for her Bobino recitals—and Georges Moustaki, who wrote much of his early material—he embarked on a singing career which would prove nothing short of magnificent. In 1971 he recorded 'Édith', a poem by Jean Dréjac. Sublimely set to music by Michel Legrand—whose father, Raymond, had arranged her 1947-8 recordings for Decca—this tells of the thrill that Reggiani experienced when he first heard Piaf sing 'La vie en rose':

> I'm sad that Piaf never heard me sing. Then again, had I been interested in the music hall back then when I first got to know her, she would have wanted to take over my life and probably made it hell for a couple of years—in the nicest way—as had happened with Yves Montand and all the others. Barbara had a much gentler, less argumentative approach. Well, as one of her confidants, I guess you already know that.

8: Charles Aznavour

■   ■   ■

It was Charles Aznavour who coined the term 'Piaf's Boys' for her lovers, and once each man had been officially recognized as such, he would be supplied with his 'uniform and accoutrements': blue serge suit and matching navy blue tie, a car—more than one, if he could not make up his mind which colour he preferred—gold cufflinks, tie-pin and cigarette lighter. And if the lover was truly special, the lighter would be platinum.

When Piaf first met Aznavour in 1948, he was one half of the Aznavour-Roche duo—which though successful, was dismissed by her as 'old-fashioned'. Upon learning that Aznavour wrote his own material, she asked him to write her a song. With his partner, Pierre Roche, he wrote her 'Il pleut', a maudlin piece which she nevertheless recorded. Shortly after Marcel Cerdan's death he presented her with 'Je hais les dimanches', which he had written with Florence Véran:

> *Tous les jours de la semaine*
> *Sont vides et sonnent le creux,*
> *Mais pire qu'la semaine y a l'dimanche prétentieux …*
> *Je hais les dimanches!*

Weekdays are empty and hollow,
But worse than the week is pretentious Sunday ...
I hate Sundays!

Piaf turned the song down, and told Aznavour, 'Give it to Juliette Gréco or Lucienne Delyle. That way they'll have a song of their own and stop stealing other people's.' Aznavour did just this, and the darling of the existentialists not only had a hit with it, it won her the newly-launched *Prix Édith Piaf.* Charles explained:

> She went crazy! Though she was always polite whenever they met, Piaf disliked Gréco intensely at this time, accusing her not just of stealing this song from her, but of stealing some of her other songs, including 'Les feuilles mortes', 'Sous le ciel de Paris', and 'Chanson de Catherine'. But she promised that she would forgive me so long as I wrote *her* something else.

There is an unwritten law of the music hall, that for the first six months of its life, a new song should be performed only by the artiste who introduced it. Though *she* had never adhered to this rule before, Piaf was forced to wait until October 1951 before recording 'Je hais les dimanches'. She did record nine other Aznavour songs, including 'Plus bleu que tes yeux', 'C'est un gars', and 'Jezebel', of which more later.

Aznavour was also roped into Piaf's provincial tour, scheduled to kick off in April 1950, which would be followed by an extensive tour of the United States and Canada. As with Michel Émer, now that he had begun writing songs for her she needed him close by to keep her supplied with fresh material as, unlike most of her contemporaries, she did not stick to the same setlist night after night.

There was also a new man, who again entered Piaf's life by way of a song. Eddie Constantine (1917-93) was a brash American, and like Marcel Cerdan appealing to look at, with a rugged pock-marked face, sexy smile and affable disposition. He was also married. Having attempted and failed to get into musicals in Hollywood, he had left his wife and small daughter, and headed for Europe, promising to return to them only after he had made a name for himself. At the Vienna Conservatoire he had won a prize for singing bass—not that this had done him much good, for he had spent the next six months doing any number of 'non-showbusiness' jobs, including washing corpses in a funeral parlour. Eventually, he had arrived in Paris, where he had earned a meagre living filling in for cancellations in the cabarets around the Left Bank. At one of these he had been 'spotted' by Lucienne Boyer—who had taken a shine to him and offered him a regular spot at her Club de l'Opéra.

While working for Boyer, Constantine had written an English lyric for 'Hymne à l'amour' which he had taken to Piaf. She accepted the song at once and, when she learned that he was working for a rival, she offered to double his salary so long as he moved to her camp. Two days later, the press reported that they were lovers ... and that Constantine would be augmenting her tour. Not only this, after the tour she would be taking him with her to America. She was still unaware that he was married, and could potentially leave her at any time and return to his family. Charles explained:

> The French tour was a nightmare. I opened the show. The rest of the time I was the dogsbody—I drove the car, ran errands, carried suitcases, and was cursed at all the time, and I loved every minute of it because all the time I was with Piaf, I was learning. Her English was not that bad, but she made him learn French, and his accent was terrible. The critics hated him, and she took it out on me.

Though he only performed three songs each evening, Aznavour had been well-received, while audiences had laughed at Constantine's lame attempts at classics such as Lucienne Boyer's 'Parlez-moi d'amour'. Yet it was Aznavour who was made to suffer when Louis Barrier's New York counterpart, Clifford Fischer, announced that Piaf had been in touch with him to say that Aznavour was 'not quite ready' for his big break, and therefore would not be included in the tour package.

Aznavour beat Piaf at her own game, for whilst she was in Ottawa she received a telegram informing her that her protégé had been interned on Ellis Island because he had travelled steerage class with no work-permit and little money. Piaf was so impressed that she cabled him the $500 he needed to bail himself out and catch up with her on the tour. Aznavour did not join her, however. His singing partner Pierre Roche happened to be in Montreal, so he joined him instead. The engagements they played here would be among their last before going their separate ways. Roche stayed on in Canada, while Aznavour turned solo.

Upon her return to Paris, Piaf opened at the ABC in the musical-comedy, *La p'tite Lili*, playing the heroine of the piece whilst Eddie Constantine portrayed a gangster. Their duet, 'C'est toi', was a big hit with audiences, but there were backstage squabbles between the American and the second lead, an up-and-coming young actor named Robert Lamoureux who would soon become a household name in France. Piaf was starting to tire of Constantine. The fact that he was always telling her that his ambition was to be reunited his family as soon as he could, made it obvious that he was only using her as a stepping-stone. She began flirting with Lamoureux. In fact, the split from Constantine happened sooner than anyone expected, when his wife flew to Paris and turned up at the theatre one evening to surprise him.

Constantine's replacement was not Lamoureux, as her friends had anticipated—but the racing-cyclist André Pousse (1919-2005). They had previously met in 1949 in New York, when romance had been out of the question on account of Cerdan. Pousse, a fitness fanatic, made Piaf aware of her own lethargy, and acting on his advice that the country air would do her good she bought a farm, Les Cérisiers, near Dreux. The venture cost her 21 million francs, and would later be sold at a loss. Their affair ended abruptly in August 1951 when the car Pousse was driving, with Piaf and Aznavour asleep in the back, skidded off the road and she ended up with several broken ribs and a fractured left arm. *La P'tite Lili* was drawing towards the end of its run, but rather than cancel the show, Piaf insisted on singing each evening, and soon became addicted to the morphine her doctor prescribed for the pain. In her memoirs, she pulled no punches when describing this dark period of her life:

> Drugs scarred me for life, and it is perhaps because
> of my drug-taking that I will doubtless die before
> my time. Friends saw me foaming at the mouth, or
> clinging to the rails of my bed. They saw me inject

myself through my skirt and stocking. Without drugs I would have been incapable of going on stage, let alone of singing—and not even the very worst of my despairs would have prevented me from singing.

Piaf's 'years of hell' had begun. Raymond Rouleau, the play's producer, closed the production down—perhaps the last thing he should have done, for with nothing to do Piaf turned even more towards the needle for solace. André Pousse deserted her while she was in the hospital and later cruelly opined, 'I was never really in love with Piaf, only with her voice. The physical side of her only made my flesh creep.' Her true friends watched over her as best they could, but she outsmarted them by hiding drugs in places they never thought of looking. In her second autobiography, *Ma vie*, published in 1963, Piaf names her 'helper'—in other words her supplier—as 'Janine'. One theory is that while she was dictating these memoirs, she changed several names on account of France's draconian laws on privacy, and that 'Janine' was actually Simone Berteaut. Pousse was replaced by his friend and fellow cycling champion, the previously mentioned Toto Gérardin—who ironically *did* drop in on Piaf whilst she was recovering from her accident.

As for Charles Aznavour, he turned solo and became a big star in France virtually overnight, and not long afterwards a worldwide sensation. He and Piaf remained close friends for the rest of her life. He recalled, with great affection:

> Piaf had a very special place in the hearts of the French people. Since Piaf, only Barbara has had that kind of standing. I adored every minute that I spent as Piaf's slave, and couldn't have had a better apprenticeship. She made me work harder than I've worked in all the years since. She was a sacred monster! I experienced her highs and lows. She had the loudest laugh I've ever heard, and the worst temper, though she never got angry with me. Everyone in Camp Piaf had to do her bidding—to eat when she ate, to sleep when she slept. If she liked a film—like *The Third Man*, which most of us found boring—she made us sit through it six times, though this allowed us to catch up on our sleep. Her parties were lavish. She was the most generous woman I've ever known. She would open her bag and give her last franc to a beggar she'd seen in the street. When she was feeling down in the dumps, to cheer herself up she would call me or Michel Émer and say, 'Hey—write me a song, and make sure you find me a new way to die'. Michel was good at that, whereas I preferred to write about being alive. She always said that 'Une enfant' was her favourite out of all the songs I wrote for her. That's because someone died at the end, in this instance an errant

child who is found dead at the side of the road, as opposed to the usual drowning, murder, electricity, car-smash, gas or routine broken heart. For me, she is not dead but living in the hearts of those of us who loved her.

9: Marlene Dietrich

■   ■   ■

Before Constantine, Pousse and Gérardin passed through the 'Piaf Production Line' there was Jean-Louis Jaubert (1920-2013), of the nine-strong Les Compagnons de la Chanson. She and Yvon Jean-Claude had appeared on the same bill as them in 1944 whilst touring Switzerland, when the *chansonnier* John Villard, aka Gilles, had offered her 'Les trois cloches'. Piaf had declined the song, denouncing is as 'too folksy', and Gilles had given it to a local singer, Édith Burger. When Piaf heard Burger singing this on the radio, she called Gilles and bawled him out for giving *her* song to a 'wailer'. She then declared that she and Les Compagnons would record the song—therefore guaranteeing its author a substantial return—so long as he ordered Burger to remove it from her repertoire. It has to be remembered just how big a name Piaf was, even then. Gilles agreed and courtesy of Piaf 'Les trois cloches' was transformed into a true *chanson-réaliste*, telling the story in everyday words of the birth, marriage and death of Jean-François Nicot in a small, provincial village:

Village au fond de la vallée,
Loin des chemins, loin des humains,
Voici qu'après dix-neuf années,
Coeur en émoi,
Jean-François prend pour femme la douce Elise ...

[A village, deep in the valley,
Far from roads and humans,
Here, after nineteen years, heart all aflutter,
Jean-François takes sweet Elise for his wife ...]

The song was a massive hit around the world—in France, it sold 60,000 copies within three weeks of its release, almost unheard of at the time. Today, especially in the English adaptation where Jean-François Nicot becomes 'Little Jimmy Brown', it is frequently regarded as kitschy, and lampooned, but in France during the summer of 1946 it was hailed as a symbol of potent patriotism and a welcome antidote to the ravages suffered under the German Occupation. The song was also included in *Neuf garçons et un Coeur*, the film which Piaf made with the group. Shot over a twelve-day period, this is a musical fantasy set one Christmas Eve. Christine (Piaf) is the leader of a hard-up group of singers. First she falls asleep and dreams that they are all in heaven, only to wake up to the harsh reality that for them, the festive season will be frugal. Then, a miracle occurs when a kindly benefactor hires them to perform in his club—Le Paradis. Attached to this easy-going plot were five songs, including 'C'est pour ça', with which Piaf sometimes opened her American recitals, and one number which almost did not make it to the soundtrack. This was 'La vie en rose', which Piaf had written for her friend, the singer Marianne Michel:

> *Quand il me prend dans ses bras,*
> *Il me parle tout bas, je vois la vie en rose!*
> *Il me dit des mots d'amour,*
> *Des mots de tous les jours,*
> *Et cà m'fait quelquechose!*

> [When he takes me in his arms,
> He speaks low to me, I see life in a rosy hue!
> He says words of love,
> Everyday words that do something to me!]

The love affair with Jaubert, however, did not last. Piaf and Les Compagnons recorded a clutch of songs, and embarked on a brief tour of Greece—where she had a fling with a young actor named Takis Menelaus, who took her for long, romantic moonlit strolls around the Acropolis, and asked her to marry him. Piaf seems to have taken the proposal seriously, until the next morning when the actor told her that he was *already* married. He then offered a compromise:

he would divorce his wife, so long as she gave up her career and stayed in Greece with him. One might only imagine what Piaf's response to *this* must have been.

Next up, Piaf embarked on the greatest challenge of her career so far—her first visit to the United States. She sailed to New York in November 1947 (with Les Compagnons, though they would not be touring with her) and opened at the Playhouse, on 48th Street. Initially, she was not a success. Several American journalists reported her to be 'looking dowdy' and suffering from 'extreme fatigue'. Effectively, they were seeing her as she actually was, in a grey twin-set and pillbox hat, when they had been expecting some Parisian lovely bedecked in furs and jewels. This was in the days before television, and though they had seen *Étoile sans lumière*—the film was still playing at one New York cinema, an astonishing forty weeks after its release—they had not assumed that she would dress like her character *off* the screen. Matters did not improve when they saw her on the stage—again they had anticipated someone like Joséphine Baker, drenched in feathers and crooning ditties like 'C'est si bon'—*not* a *maladive* little woman clad in black, singing songs of despair, death and lost love in a language they could not understand. The critics eschewed writing about her voice to denounce the way she looked, one observing, 'Édith Piaf wears far too much mascara, and there is so much lipstick, she looks like she is dribbling tomato juice!'

To cope with her failure—something she had not had to deal with since the Leplée affair—Piaf hired a Master of Ceremonies who explained to the audience what each song was about. This, however, completely ruined the continuity of her recitals. Then, when she was ready to throw in the towel, she was championed on the front page of the *Herald Tribune* by Virgil Thomson (1896-1989), the legendary critic and composer who that year had received the *Légion d'honneur* from the French government. His lengthy piece concluded:

> Miss Piaf presents the art of the chansonnière at its most classical. The vocalism is styled and powerful. Her diction is clarity itself … She is a great artiste because she gives you a clear vision of the scene or subject she is depicting, with a minimum injection of personality. Such a concentration at once of professional authority and of personal modesty is no end impressive …

It was largely due to this article that Piaf was offered an eight-engagement contract with the Versailles, one of New York's most exclusive cabarets, situated at 151 East 40th Street. On the night of her premiere here, she objected to the unlucky green curtains—on subsequent visits to the establishment these would be kept open so that she would not see them whilst singing. She was 'mounted' on a wooden platform to enable those at the back of the auditorium to see her, and proved so popular that her season was extended—to five months, on a salary of $1,000 a week. Over the next twelve years, the venue would act as her first port-of-call whenever she crossed the Atlantic, while just about every major star in America clamoured to be photographed with her. Some of these sniggered behind her back, finding her 'quaint', though with the exception of Bette Davis, Rock Hudson, Joan Crawford, Danny Kaye, Tallulah Bankhead and Patti Page—whose shows she appeared in—and a mere handful of others, her fame and lasting popularity by far outlived theirs. Wearing none of the fineries associated with their world, and almost always her black dress, she comes across as infinitely more glamorous and certainly more sincere than any of the 'posers' in these pictures. Judy Garland was an exception, for in some pictures they almost look like sisters. And only one of these superstars genuinely touched her heart: Marlene Dietrich.

Two women, on the face of it with little in common other than the songs they shared: 'La vie en rose', 'When The World Was Young'—and 'Un coin tout bleu', the one which Piaf had given to Damia, and which Marlene sang but never got around to recording. Marlene devoted two pages of her 1984 (French) autobiography to her close friendship with Piaf, whom she 'adopted' when the singer was at an all-time low:

She was a fragile bird, but she was also the Jezebel
with an insatiable thirst for love which compensated
for her self-confessed ugliness … I stopped being
faithful when she began taking drugs. I knew my
limits. It was like I was banging my head against
a brick wall. My love for her remained intact, but
it had become useless. I abandoned her like a lost
child. It is something that I will always regret.

And of Marlene, Piaf wrote:

Marlene was so perfect, it was hard to believe that
she actually ate. She is the most perfect woman that
I've ever had the good fortune to meet. When she
saw me downcast, worried, near breaking-point, she
made it her duty to help and encourage me, taking
care never to leave me alone with my thoughts …
Because of her I faced my problems and overcame
them. I have much to thank her for …

In 1936, Piaf had recorded 'Il n'est pas distingué'. In this,
performed in an almost incomprehensible vernacular, her
'undistinguished' friend, Zidor, tells of how he sleeps in
his hovel, fantasizing that Marlene is one of his regulars,
until for some reason Hitler enters the equation, whence
his erection subsides. Then, dreaming that he has Hitler 'on
the mat', he is not frightened of there being another war
because he remembers what happened during the last one:

Mégalomane pathétique!
Moi, Hitler je l'ai dans l'blair,
Et j'peux pas l'renifler!
Les Nazis ont l'air d'oublier
Que c'est nous dans la bagarre
Qu'on les a dérouillés!

[Pathetic megalomaniac!
I've got Hitler by the brush and can't smell him!
The Nazis tend to forget
That *we* knocked the rust off them in the brawl!]

This song had been banned during the Occupation, and was the reason Marlene had refused to attend Piaf's recitals when visiting Paris. By November 1947, however, she was not feeling quite so bitter because she had been given a copy of Piaf's recording of 'La vie en rose', and wanted to sing the song herself. In a rare act of devotion, Marlene gave Piaf a precious gift—a tiny gold cross set with seven emeralds, which she would wear for the rest of her life.

Other than in her autobiography, Marlene *never* spoke about Piaf to anyone until 1990, when she opened up to me—having changed her mind about what she had written earlier:

Everyone *thought* Piaf was a fragile little bird, but such a thing could not have been further from the truth—though she wasn't at all like that horrible caricature in the play [Pam Gems' *Piaf*]. She and I spent a lot of time together at the beginning of 1948. I'd finished making *Foreign Affair* and a film I don't even care to remember [*Jigsaw*], so I had all the time in the world to help her with her American career. One of our first conversations was about 'La vie en rose' …

Piaf had written the song which introduced her work to American audiences in 1945—while sitting in a Parisian restaurant with her friend, the singer Marianne Michel. Unable to find a pen and paper to jot down the words which had suddenly come into her head, she had grabbed Michel's eyebrow-pencil and scribbled the words to 'Les choses en roses' on the tablecloth, and when Michel had recorded it, the title had been changed to 'La vie en rose'. Roland Gerbeau, the crooner lover of Charles Trenet, had recorded a cover version. Marlene went on:

> Édith couldn't stand the man. She told me, 'Every time I heard him singing my song on the radio, I wanted to rush out of the room and throw up. I started wishing that I'd never written the fucking thing.' Édith believed in those days that she was not glamorous enough to be singing romantic songs. She was forever calling herself ugly and insecure, yet such was her charisma that she could have any

man she wanted, and usually did. One evening at the Versailles she made a play for John Garfield, a man who really did have one hell of an inflated ego. One night after one of her parties at the Waldorf Astoria I escorted her up to her room. And there he was, drunk and stark naked on her bed. Édith didn't have much English in those days, but what she knew was very colourful … After she'd given him a piece of her mind, we manhandled him out of the room and threw him right down the stairs. Ha—he was still there when I went up to her room the next morning.

When reporters questioned Piaf about this incident, she replied honestly—that all too often the man of the moment saw only the words 'Édith PIAF' in big lights above the bed, and that in many instances once he had attained a certain 'status' and she had outlived her usefulness, he had dumped her. Years later, she reflected in an interview with *France Dimanche*:

> My lifestyle was such in those days that I was taken as an easy lay. Amongst my entourage I was the good time had by all. Men treated me like a territory which had to be conquered—even though deep inside I still felt pure and desperate, far different from my degrading image. Love has always run away from me. I never kept the man

of my life in my arms for very long. Sometimes it's over nothing—a word out of place, or some unimportant lie, and my lover vanishes. Then I pray that a miracle will lead me into other arms …

Soon after meeting Marlene, Édith embarked on what she always regarded as her most important and cherished love affair—with World Middleweight Champion boxer, Marcel Cerdan, thirty-three when they met, and married with children, not that this had ever stopped her in the past. She observed in her memoirs:

> Before him, I was nothing—morally, I was a lost cause. I believed life had no meaning, that all men were beasts and that the best thing to do was have fun and do silly things, whilst waiting for death to arrive as quickly as possible. He took away that sour taste of hopelessness which had poisoned me, body and soul. He enabled me to discover that sweetness, serenity and tenderness really did exist. He lit up my world.

Piaf was writing retrospectively, in the wake of the tragedy which had brought their affair to an abrupt end—as opposed to allowing it to run its course, which it most likely would have done, had Cerdan lived. Born in Algeria in July 1916, he had begun his boxing career in Morocco, and was nicknamed 'The Moroccan Bomber'. Piaf had first met him in Paris in 1946, and is said to have found him unattractive. He was a stocky man, not much above average height, with a tough face which, when he smiled, revealed a mouthful of gold fillings and gave him the 'lived-in' look. He remains France's most famous fighter, something which is unlikely to change on account of his association with Piaf. They met again in December 1947, at a cocktail party hosted by Marlene Dietrich and Charles Boyer for French stars 'exiled' in America, at the Versailles after Piaf's show. This time, they fell in love. Cerdan was in New York to train for a fight, and was being given a tough time by the fans of his opponent, while Piaf was having a hard time getting audiences to adapt to her.

Cerdan's entourage disapproved of Piaf and declared her bad for his image as a family man. She reacted to this, when they returned to France, by asking him to introduce her to his wife, Marinette. Not only did the two women get along inordinately well, Piaf became unofficial godmother to the Cerdans' three sons, one of whom, Marcel Cerdan Jr., later played his father in the film *Édith et Marcel*. Even more astonishingly, she then forked out nineteen-million francs for a town-house at 5 rue de Gambetta, in the Bois de Boulogne—the first time she had owned a place of her own, and money she could ill afford—telling friends that

Cerdan *would* move in with her, eventually, even if it meant him moving his family in with him.

On 2 September 1948, Cerdan fought the biggest bout of his career—the World Middleweight Championship against Tony Zale—at New Jersey's Roosevelt Stadium. This coincided with Piaf's new season at the Versailles. The fight was a tough one, but Zale hit the canvas in the twelfth round, and Cerdan won the title. In March 1949, he flew to London, where he fought and beat Dick Turpin at Earls Court. Piaf accompanied him, on the first of her three brief visits to Britain. While she was here, Bernard Delfont and several other leading agents had offered her a vast fee to sing at the London Palladium, which she turned down, claiming that she had had a tough enough time winning the Americans over without having to put herself through the mill again for audiences who might not appreciate her. By way of a compromise, she gave two private, ten-song recitals at the Mayfair Hotel. These opened with 'La vie en rose', and closed with 'Tous les amoureux chantent', a number which has to be heard to be believed, for it tells of a pair of young lovers who are mown down by a car on their wedding-day. In between was 'Miserable in mink', the English version of 'Pour moi toute seule', which would be covered by the British comedienne, Dora Bryan.

At around this time, Cerdan played himself in *L'homme aux mains d'argile*, loosely based on his life. Cerdan wanted Piaf to sing in the film, but was overruled by his manager, Lucien Roupp, who could not stand her, having accused her of coming between Cerdan and his family, which she never did. Instead, she sang André Bernheim's 'Paris' over the titles, an evocative ode to the joy brought about by loving this man:

> *Un soir d'hiver, un frais visage,*
> *La Seine, un marchand de marrons,*
> *Une chambre au cinquième étage,*
> *Les café-crèmes du matin …*

> [A wintry evening, a fresh complexion,
> The Seine, a chestnut-seller,
> A room on the fifth floor,
> Creamed coffees in the morning …]

Nine months after winning his title, Cerdan returned to New York to defend it against Jake LaMotta, and lost. A rematch was scheduled for December. Piaf would be flying out for her third tour of America, which would coincide with the fight. Cerdan, who hated flying, agreed to follow on by ship. At the last moment, he changed his plans and on 27 October caught the early flight from Orly. Seven hours later, after failing to make two landings on São Miguel

Island, in the Azores, they crashed into Mount Rodonta, killing all forty-eight people on board, including the great French violinist Ginette Neveu and her pianist brother, Jean-Paul. Marlene remembered that awful day only too well:

> Only two people were capable of breaking that kind of news to her—myself and her manager [Louis Barrier], who had time to get there only because Édith always slept in until the middle of the afternoon, then rehearsed or received friends until it was time to go onstage. Everyone put on an act until he arrived. God above, she went crazy with grief. I was terrified of leaving her side for a moment … As an act of penance, she cut her hair—I still have the scissors—and she shut herself up in her room until she received a call saying that Cerdan's body had been found. It was a terrible thing to have to watch her suffer.

Piaf mourned Cerdan for the rest of her life—she wrote one of her most celebrated songs, 'Hymne à l'amour', in his memory, her theory being that it is possible to love someone *so* much that it does not matter if they die, so long as one might die too:

> *Nous aurons pour nous l'éternité,*
> *Dans le bleu de toute l'immensité,*

Dans le ciel, plus de problèmes.
Dieu réunit ceux qui s'aiment!

[We will have eternity to ourselves,
In the blue immensity of heaven
No more problems.
God unites those who loved!]

Piaf had a show the evening she was told of Cerdan's death. Marlene and Louis Barrier begged her to cancel, but she refused. She wrote in her memoirs:

> The dreadful news knocked me senseless. I suffered
> a martyrdom onstage that night. I was like a corpse,
> a mortally wounded soul. Yet I was able to hang on
> until the end, and I told them, 'Tonight I'm singing
> for Marcel Cerdan. I'm singing for him alone.'

Only days after Cerdan's death, Piaf participated in a radio link-up between New York and Paris, and stunned listeners by announcing that with Cerdan dead, she too wanted to die. The response was tremendous—thousands of fans begged her with one voice not to do it. Even the radio announcer told her that she had no right to leave them in such a manner. Piaf belonged to the people! She was an international monument. This brought her to her senses. From now on she would *live* for Cerdan, though her closest friends knew that from now on, it would almost certainly be a living death.

Taking into consideration the pattern she had set for herself, there is little doubt that, had Cerdan lived, their relationship would have petered out like all the others. He had already made it clear to her that for his children's sakes he would never divorce his wife. So why, the cynics may ask, did he remain the greatest love of her life? The answer is so very simple: because he died at the very zenith of their affair—without giving Piaf the eventual opportunity of walking out on *him*, once their ardour had started to cool and she had found a suitable replacement.

In the wake of Marcel Cerdan's death, Piaf's life rapidly descended into a downward spiral of alcohol and drugs. Oblivion in the face of such tragedy was her way of trying to cope with the grief. She sought solace in the arms of men, who, rather than trying to help, matched her glass for glass.

After Cerdan there were a number of others, until along came the man who was regarded by many of her friends as her greatest mistake.

Jacques Pills (René Ducos, 1906-70) was the popular singer, formerly one half of the duo, Pills and Tabet, who had a big hit with the song, 'Couchés dans le foin', recorded in English as 'Lazing in the Hay' by Bing Crosby. His and Piaf's paths had crossed several times over the years, and like Cerdan he appears to have been a 'slow-burner' until appearing with Piaf on a New York radio show where the host, impressed by his flashy smile, casual manner and romantic interpretations of songs such as 'Cheveux dans le vent', had introduced him as 'Monsieur Charm'. In May 1952, Pills charmed Piaf by bringing her a song, 'Je t'ai dans la peau' (I've got you inside my skin). It was the sexiest and most suggestive song she ever sang, a clear forerunner to the Gainsbourg-Birkin duets of the early Seventies—one only has to observe her performing it in the film, *Boum sur Paris*, to make the comparison. Set to music by his pianist, François Silly, who later achieved world fame as Gilbert Bécaud, the song resurrected Pills' flagging career, particularly when Édith took advantage of this being a Leap Year and asked him to marry her.

Jacques Pills was an opportunist. He was involved with Joséphine Baker when Piaf proposed, and it was reported at the time that before giving her his response, he called Joséphine, working in New York, with the ultimatum, 'Marry me, or I'll marry Piaf!' He also lied to Piaf about his age. In her memoirs she calls him her 'rock', but he was anything but.

The civil ceremony took place in Paris on 29 July 1952, at the Mairie of the 16th arrondissement. For Édith, it was not a true wedding since it lacked church bells and a choir, and she refused to wear her wedding ring until it had been properly blessed. Therefore the 'real' ceremony took place in New York, at the Church of St-Vincent-de-Paul, on 20 September. The witnesses were Louis Barrier—and Marlene, who despite her fondness for Édith took a great deal of persuading to attend, as she explained:

> The first time I met Jacques Pills, I took an immediate dislike to him. That man was too *charming* for his own good, and it was all put on. Because she pleaded with me and because I loved her so very much, I gave in. That day I kept looking at her, hoping she would be capable of staying on her feet. She was very happy, but very sick also. I had arranged everything—her hair and her make-up, and the bunch of white roses which she carried. She seemed lost, like a little child … And I remember saying to myself, 'I hope this is going to work out for her,' though I knew that it never would.

Piaf wore a full-length, pleated pale blue gown and violet tulle hat—in the photographs, she declared, she would *look* as if she was dressed in white. The press reported that she had paid $700 for the ensemble, from Saks of Madison Avenue—also that she may have taken something to calm her nerves. Marlene laughed at this:

The dress *was* from the store on Madison Avenue, but it was my wedding gift to her. I didn't buy him anything. Knowing him, he would probably have sold it ... Yes, she was very nervous before the ceremony—but nothing that a couple of sips from my hip flask couldn't cure.

What cynics found amusing was that, on the eve of the civil ceremony in Paris, Piaf had asked Michel Émer to write her a song to celebrate her forthcoming nuptials. He gave her 'Jean et Martine', a woeful piece which tells of a young woman who is preparing dinner for her lorry driver husband when someone comes to the door to tell her that he has been killed, and that now she must prepare for his funeral. This song was recorded on 3 September, along with two others: Gilbert Bécaud's 'Les croix', a very dramatic piece in which the narrator has an immense cross of lead within her head, engraved with the word 'SUFFERING', so heavy to carry that she feels she will die from the effort; and 'Bravo Pour Le Clown', in which the clown, nagged by his despotic wife, kills her by throwing her from the top of the circus tent, and ends up in a lunatic asylum.

Returning to Paris, Piaf and Pills rented a plush new apartment at 67-bis boulevard Lannes, an opulent quarter overlooking the Bois de Boulogne—she added the 'bis' because the two numbers totalled an unlucky thirteen, and *she* footed all the bills. The apartment would remain her home for the rest of her life, and yet she never really moved in. There were nine rooms, but for her the only ones of importance were the kitchen, her bedroom, the bathroom and the vast, ballroom-sized lounge which saw most of the action—gatherings, receptions, endless parties. She installed a grand piano, tables which were constantly cluttered with bottles, glasses and manuscripts, and dozens of armchairs and divans were scattered about the place for members of her entourage who could not keep up with her to flop into. Her clothes and other effects were kept in trunks and chests—as she was always on the move, she saw no point in unpacking them.

The Piaf-Pills union was doomed from the start. Piaf, always in search of the security which had evaded her, had drifted uncompromisingly from one man to the next. Each relationship had been more intense and exhausting (for both parties) than the last. This was the secret of her success as a singer: had her personal life been less dramatic and complicated, there would have been fewer good songs because much of her repertoire was directly influenced by her experiences. Pills, with his cheesy mannerisms, air of self-importance and sycophantic charm, was too weak to handle her. He found it easier to turn a blind eye to her increasing addiction to codeine and morphine … and encouraged her to drink even more, even when she told him that she had booked herself into a rehabilitation clinic. Marlene recalled:

> Édith needed an iron hand to guide her back on to the rails, a man who genuinely cared about her, and not for what he was getting out of her. Pills knew his career was over but he hung on because of the money. Afterwards, Édith told me that she had told him she was taking drugs on account of her rheumatism, and that he had believed her. Now, that man was anything but stupid. He knew what she was doing, and he did *nothing* to stop her because his own career was finished and she was paying for everything. I told her, 'Get rid of that son-of-a-bitch and find yourself a *real* husband!'

Marlene was not the only one to tell her that she was wasting her time. In an attempt to save her marriage, Piaf announced that she was reviving *Le bel indifférent*, with Pills in the part which Paul Meurisse had played so well, theoretically perfect casting since he had played more or less an extension of his surly, arrogant self. Louis Barrier advised her that this was a bad idea. Such was Pills's ego that he demanded the same salary for himself as Piaf, and the theatres announced that they wanted nothing to do with the project. Piaf was forced to personally hire the Théâtre

Marigny, at the bottom of the Champs-Elysées. Pills proved hopeless and on at least one occasion was booed when walking up to the front of the stage to take his bow, but audiences tolerated the play—or hung around the vestibule until it was finished—because it took up only the first half of the bill, with Piaf performing twenty songs after the interval … closing with 'Bravo pour le clown'.

Marlene also recalled an amusing incident, which occurred early in 1956, during Piaf's extended American tour, when the two of them were invited to a party hosted by Orson Welles—at the Waldorf Astoria in New York, where the incident with John Garfield had taken place:

> We were playing that game where you have to tie a scarf around your eyes and catch somebody [Blind Man's Buff]. Then whoever had been caught had to hand over a hundred-dollar bill for Orson Welles' charity. There was this actor called John Glendale. I'd never seen him before. Édith said he was the spitting image of John Garfield. We spun her around and she caught him—but he shoved something else into her hand instead of the money. Many of the guests were shocked, but Édith just laughed and told him, 'Honey, that's the smallest dick I've ever handled!' She told me afterwards that she'd had an affair with him, but it could only have been for that one night because she spent the whole

of the next day with me, and we never saw John Glendale again. Then a few nights later we went to another party and we sang a dirty version of one of her songs. Someone told me that it had been taped, God help us.

The song was 'Mon légionnaire', where the line 'Il m'a aimé toute la nuit' (He loved me all night long) became 'Il m'a foutré toute la nuit (He fucked me all night long). And what Marlene did not add was that, after performing the song, Piaf had fallen on the floor and begun crossing the room on all fours while 'barking' at her astonished audience, in English, 'I am a dog!'—at which point Marlene had borrowed a belt from one of the waiters, placed it around Piaf's neck and scolded, 'Don't you *dare* bite anyone, you vicious little beast!' In her memoirs, while discussing the one-night stand with John Glendale, Piaf attempted to save Marlene's blushes by naming the 'dog-handler' as Ginette Richer, her *frangine* who sometimes accompanied her on her travels.

But, *did* Marlene wash her hands of Piaf, as she had observed in her memoirs? There were certainly lots of pictures of them together after this time. She explained:

> I never really *abandoned* Piaf. I wrote that, I know. The truth is, Édith's husband asked me to stay away from her. And that's what I did. And we *always* kept

in touch on the telephone, or I would drop in at her apartment when Pills was not around. She always sounded or *looked* so strong and I thought she'd got over her problems. Obviously, she hadn't, and there were always plenty of hangers-on to complicate matters.

Marlene was also witness to Piaf's rage, in the Spring of 1960, when her manager Louis Barrier was contacted by the British impresario, Bunny Lewis, who offered Piaf 'a phenomenal fee' for just one concert in London. Though very ill, it appears that she *would* have come to Britain, had Lewis—who also wrote songs for the likes of Helen Shapiro and David Whitfield—not sent her a tape of his latest 'masterpiece', an English adaptation of 'Milord', recounted from the man's point of view, performed by Frankie Vaughan. If anything, his inferior version of the song, which reached Number 34 in the charts, only drew more attention to the Piaf version, which entered the Top 20, in those days extremely unusual for a song performed in a foreign language (in Germany, it was the biggest selling record of the year)—and her only British chart hit. Marlene explained:

> I can't remember how much he offered, only that it was a lot. I advised her to accept but Édith took it as a personal insult. She told me, 'It's a *woman's*

song, for God's sake. What the hell does *he* know about being a whore? If that's all the respect the British have for my work, I'm *never* going there.

Inasmuch as she had loathed Jacques Pills, neither was Marlene initially over-enamoured of Piaf's second husband, Théo Sarapo. The civil ceremony took place at the Mairie of the 16th arrondissement of Paris on 9 October 1962, and was followed by a religious one at the Greek Orthodox Church on rue Daru. Marlene was invited, and Piaf asked her over the phone, but on both occasions politely declined.

> I had last seen Édith at Thionville, during her so-called suicide tour. It was her forty-fifth birthday, and though she was still very sick, she seemed to be coping with her problems because there was no man around to complicate matters. I still loved her very much, but felt that she should have learned her lesson with Pills. She called me and said, 'We're what you might call a nonconformist Romeo and Juliet.' He [Théo] was a nice young man, but I always thought he married her for her money. I later found out that he didn't. But he was also a homosexual, and I couldn't condone that.

Marlene *did* eventually accept Théo, when she realized that all he would actually inherit from Piaf, as per Gallic law, would be a mountain of debts because she had always lived way beyond her means. Marlene never left Théo's side for one moment on the day of Édith's funeral, and accompanied him back to Boulevard Lannes, her apartment for the last eight years of her life, where she promised to keep in touch:

> I would have stayed longer, but I had to prepare for Cocteau's funeral, the next day. And Édith's death had affected me badly. As you know, I myself was busy travelling around the world with my own stage show, so there wasn't much time for us to meet during that last year. Thank God for the telephone. And thank God for that young man, who *had* been good for her, after all. He and I spoke many times on the telephone, and in the end I grew to like him. But two funerals in as many days was more than anyone could bear, and after embracing the second widow [Jean Marais, Cocteau's long-time partner] I came to the conclusion that the next funeral I would be going to would be my own.

10: Irene Bevan

Irene Bevan (1914-96) was Gracie Fields' stepdaughter, and for a time worked as Joséphine Baker's personal assistant, while Joséphine was involved with Jacques Pills. She recalled how, years after the event, Joséphine would still be 'ranting and raving' over the dreadful way Pills had treated her, and confirmed what Marlene had said of this man:

> Jacques Pills was an opportunist, homosexual by inclination, whose *truc* was preying on famous women. He used Joséphine like a stepping-stone, then dropped her like a hot brick once his own career got under way. Her every move was vetted by him. He handled her bookings and contracts, and her money, much of which went into his own pocket. When he finally married Lucienne Boyer, he went around boasting that theirs was a marriage made in heaven, yet he was never faithful to her and it ended in divorce. It's easy to understand how such a charlatan could have pulled the wool over Piaf's eyes. Like Joséphine she was astonishingly naïve where men were concerned, though by the time she got around to him she'd had more than her share of men and she should have known better. Thankfully, when she realized what kind of man he was, she dropped him like a hot brick.

11: Dorothy Squires

■   ■   ■

At a party in Hollywood, not long after marrying Jacques Pills, Édith was introduced to my very good friend Dorothy Squires (1918-98), arguably Britain's greatest equivalent of a *chanteuse-réaliste*, and at the time married to the up-and-coming actor, Roger Moore. During the late Forties, Dot had a number of massive hits penned for her by her then-partner, Billy Reid. Édith had imported her recordings from England, and had seriously considered having 'I'll Close My Eyes' adapted into French. Dot recalled:

> For some reason, my records couldn't be released in America, so other artists covered my British hits— Margaret Whiting topped the American charts with 'A Tree In The Meadow', and Eddie Fisher with 'I'm Walking Behind You'. In the strength of this, I moved to Los Angeles and worked a lot on the cabaret circuit. One evening, I introduced 'If You Love me, Really Love Me', the English version of 'Hymne à l'amour'. I'd met Piaf briefly at a party a few weeks earlier, and had no idea that she was in the audience. When she walked into my dressing room I was terrified—even more so when she told

me that she didn't care for my arrangement of her song. Then, before I could offer my excuses she said, in broken English, 'But you've got a lovely voice. Don't worry, I'll write an arrangement for you myself.' And that's exactly what she did.

Piaf had already recorded 'Hymn a l'amour' in English—as 'Hymn To Love', with lyrics by Eddie Constantine. After hearing Dorothy Squires singing the far superior lyrics, she dropped the Constantine adaptation and introduced the new one—her own—on *The Ed Sullivan Show*:

There was nothing elaborate or big band about it— just a sincere and heartfelt arrangement which I put into my show at once, and recorded the following year. Piaf never did a studio version, so far as I was aware. Then, a few years after her death I did my own arrangement of 'If You Love Me, Really Love Me', and included it in the autograph sequence in my concerts. Piaf really did hold the audience in the palm of her tiny hand. I also learned a lot from her about lighting, and years later when I was hiring the halls myself, and [was] effectively my own boss, I put all she had taught me to good use. I believe that along with Judy Garland, she's by far the best woman singer this world has ever known.

12: Peggy Lee

■   ■   ■

Piaf recorded Philippe-Gérard's 'Le chevalier de Paris' in June 1950, and sang it until 1952, when it won the prestigious *Grand Prix du Disque*, whence she dropped it, claiming that the fuss had over-commercialized it. Therefore when presented with an English adaptation of the song, 'When The World Was Young', she suggested that it should be offered to Peggy Lee or Patti Page, two singers she admired—she had appeared on the latter's television show. Page declined the song, for no other reason than if Piaf could not sing it, then neither would she. Piaf then collaborated with the lyricist William Engvick and wrote her 'I Remember Today'. Released in September 1957, this was a big hit in America, and in Britain was covered by Anne Shelton and Ruby Murray.

Prior to this, Piaf recorded 'Si tu partais', the first of her songs to be translated into English:

> *Si un jour tu partais sans retour,*
> *Les fleurs perdraient leur parfum,*
> *Et ce serait la fin de toute joie,*
> *Reste avec moi, car je mourrais si tu partais!*

[If one day you left without returning,
The flowers would lose their perfume,
And it would be the end of all joy,
Stay with me, for I would die if you left!]

This song had come about courtesy of Piaf's fling with Takis Menelaus, in Athens in 1946, when the young actor is said to have wept on her shoulder after showing her the Acropolis by moonlight, and told her, 'If you left and never came back, there'd be no more joy in my life and I would die.' Piaf had related the story to Michel Émer, and in the space of twenty-four hours he had presented her with this beautiful piece. The English adaptation with lyrics by Geoffrey Parsons, who also wrote 'If You Love Me, Really Love Me' came to be when, during a visit to America, Piaf attended a Frankie Laine concert and heard him singing 'Jezebel'—*before* he recorded it. She was so bowled over by this that she asked Charles Aznavour, with her at the time, to write her a French lyric. He did this, but for once Piaf obeyed '*le loi du music-hall*'. Laine recorded his version of 'Jezebel' in April 1951, and she recorded hers in November. And when Geoffrey Parsons presented her with 'If You Go', she promptly gave this to Frankie Laine—who put it into his repertoire, but did not record it until 1958, when he sang it in French. There was also an excellent cover version by British Forces sweetheart, Vera Lynn.

In June 1961 Peggy recorded the song in a new arrangement by Quincy Jones, who considered it so important that he decided to use it as the title for her new album. As Piaf had recorded the original for Decca in February 1947—during the twenty month interim period between her Polydor and Pathé-Marconi contracts—it had not been widely distributed, and Peggy had recorded it knowing nothing of its background, as she explained:

Had I known it was Piaf's song, I would have asked her permission to sing it. Then I heard on the grapevine that she may have been displeased with me because she had also sung 'All The Apple Trees' ['When The World Was Young']. I didn't know that either. So I *asked* her if I could do 'If You Go', and she replied that if I did, it would be a great honour for her. Coming from a great lady like her, *I* was the one who felt honoured. We also were both very privileged to have recorded two of Jerry Leiber's and Mike Stoller's finest songs—Piaf did 'Black Denim Trousers and Motorcycle Boots' ('L'homme a la moto') and I did 'Is That All There Is?' I can well imagine her singing my song—though could you imagine the reaction from my fans, if I'd have sung the other one about the man in the leather jacket ending up under the wheels of the Southern Express. Now *that* would have been great fun.

13: Catherine Jan

■　　　■　　　■

By the end of 1954, Piaf's 'years of hell' were more or less behind her, though she still had some way to go as far as her drug and drink problems were concerned. Then, quite unexpectedly, Louis Barrier secured her a contract with the Paris Olympia, where she would ascend to previously unimagined heights. Between the turn of the century and 1928, when it had been turned into a cinema, the biggest names in France had appeared here. In 1954 it was taken over by Bruno Coquatrix, an old acquaintance of Piaf who would transform it into the most prestigious music hall in France, a position it retains to this day. There are some critics who believe that an *artiste* is not worthy of being deemed thus until they have appeared at the Olympia.

Initially, Coquatrix had hesitated before booking Piaf, until Louis Barrier convinced him that Jacques Pills was out of her life for good. He took a risk and signed her up for one month, twice the length of a normal contract. She opened in January 1955, only to prove beyond doubt that she was the hottest property in Europe. There was exciting new material by Henri Contet and Marguerite Monnot, and revivals of 'L'accordéoniste' and 'Je n'en connais pas la fin', and she introduced 'La Goualante du Pauvre Jean', which became a massive hit around the world. Piaf championed whores in 'C'est à Hambourg' and Jesus in 'Soeur Anne'. She confessed her carnal sins in 'Mea Culpa', declaring that for love she would commit them all again. She brought the house down with 'Miséricorde', a rare political statement for Piaf about a woman who has lost her lover to the horrors of war:

> Les beaux rêves sont gratuits,
> Moi, le seule qui me reste
> C'est l'odeur de sa veste quand j'dansais avec lui …
> Et la vie est si moche,
> Que même ça je l'oublierai …

> [Beautiful dreams are free,
> For me all that remains
> Is the odour of his jacket when I danced with him …
> And life is so lousy that I'll forget …]

In January 1956, after a 'man-free' year and in the wake of an exhaustive tour of North America, Piaf was the first popular singer to appear at Carnegie Hall. This was her first legitimate one-woman show, within which she was the only artiste on the bill, with an interval dividing the twenty-seven songs. In May she returned to the Olympia, where in an astonishing three-month run she broke every conceivable attendance record—the theatre even contravened fire regulations by setting up folding seats in the aisles. The recording of the premiere sold 20,000 copies within two weeks of its release. Piaf's new songs included 'Marie la Française', about the French girl whose mother believes she is doing well in Australia, until she learns, when attending her funeral, that she has been working as a prostitute; and 'Soudain une vallée', an adaptation by Jean Dréjac of the American song, 'Suddenly There's A Valley', which Piaf sang but never got around to recording in English. Dréjac also adapted 'Black Denim Trousers And Motorcycle Boots'—it became 'L'homme à la moto' and was such a big hit that the original version was soon forgotten. It tells the ubiquitous story of the leather-clad demon who, with his girlfriend Mary-Lou, attempts to outrace the Southern express, and fails. Piaf's greatest success at Olympia '56 was 'Les amants d'un jour'. It tells the story of young lovers so misunderstood that their only way out is suicide in a tawdry room, and is so sensitively narrated by the woman who washes glasses at the back of the café that the tragedy becomes a working-class Mayerling of considerable romanticism and beauty. One is instantly reminded of those little French tourist-class hotels with never-ending spiral staircases, sagging beds, cracked sinks and peeling wallpaper, yet with unmistakable qualities of their own:

> On les a trouvés se tenant par la main,
> Les yeux refermés, vers d'autres matins.
> Remplis de soleil, on les a couchés,
> Unis et tranquilles, dans un lit creusé ...

> [They found them hand in hand,
> Their eyes closed towards other mornings.
> In the sunshine, they laid them to rest,
> Peacefully together, in a hollow bed ...]

After the Olympia, Piaf returned to America for another extensive tour, and a second appearance at Carnegie Hall where she sang 'Les amants d'un jour' in English, and raised the roof with 'Les grognards', a veritable masterpiece which opens with the marching of feet and a spoken verse: 'The grumblers have no guns, no grenades, no shoes. They are the ghosts of Napoleon's soldiers who are haunting Paris because, in life, they never got to see it.'

Piaf was now the highest-paid female entertainer in the world, and despite divorcing Jacques Pills smack in the middle of this triumphant period, her life was more settled than it had been for some time because there was no regular man around to complicate matters. This changed when she returned to France to begin preparing for Olympia '58, which would be preceded by a lengthy provincial tour. Catherine Jan travelled with her—just as she needed the songwriter of the moment with her at all times, as Charles Aznavour and Michel Émer testified, so Piaf needed her clairvoyant close at hand. Catherine recalled Piaf's sense of humour. As with Damia and Barbara, though the songs were dramatic and morbid at times, the woman herself was far from miserable:

> When Piaf laughed, everyone had to laugh. That was one of the rules of the household—but Piaf's laugh was very genuine, and so loud it would have demolished a building from two-hundred metres. She was also a great practical joker, though some of the tricks she played on people were a little juvenile—such as spiking someone's coffee with Epsom salts, or emptying shampoo into the lavatory cistern—or in the case of Félix Marten, hiding a dead fish in the engine of his car, though that was actually an act of revenge because the man was *so* arrogant.

Catherine recalled Piaf's taste in men, and two men in particular. In the past, she had always chosen her own *vedette-américaine*, and frequently the other artistes on the bill, but in this instance she left the choice to Bruno

Coquatrix. 'I trust his judgement,' she said in one interview. 'If Coquatrix hired a deaf mute to sing *Tosca*, it'd be fine by me.' He chose German-born Félix Marten (1919-92), who had arrived in Paris before the war hoping for a career in films, only to change direction and take up singing when acting had not worked out as planned. Marten possessed a distinct nasal quality which suited the numbers he was preparing to sing at the Olympia—'T'as une belle cravate' and 'Fais moi un checque' were cynical but melodious, with a speedy delivery—but when he slowed down to perform the kind of romantic songs that Piaf had in mind, he tended to go way off-key. His stance was also ungainly, as Montand's had been in his early days: conscious of his great height—6'5"—he had the tendency to stoop over the microphone, arms akimbo like some gigantic bird of prey. Marten had recently had a hit with 'La Marie-vison'. Piaf had complained to friends that she was sick to death of hearing it on the radio. Her first regular man since her divorce from Jacques Pills, he was a good deal more handsome than his last few predecessors and knew it. Piaf once remarked that he was *so* vain, that he should have married his mirror. Catherine recalled:

> Of the men, the worst two that I remember meeting were Georges Moustaki and Félix Marten, a singer so up himself, you wouldn't believe it. He was booked

to appear with her at the Olympia, and without being properly introduced he barged into her dressing-room during rehearsals and announced, 'Hi, Édith. I'm Félix Marten.' Without looking up, she replied, 'Hi, Félix. I'm Édith Piaf. Fuck off!' Then he gave her the most beautiful song you could imagine—'Je me souviens d'une chanson'. She fell in love with him—and decided she would mould him into a star, as she had Montand. He was tremendously good looking—but on stage he just stood there like a lump of wood, and one evening Piaf was so annoyed with this that she shouted from the wings, 'Give it your best shot, like I told you to, and you'll even have the men coming in their pants.' Then she found out that he'd told a reporter that he found her repulsive in bed, and that he was only sleeping with her to boost his career. I'll never forget what happened next. She called a meeting, on the stage of the Olympia, just moments before curtain up and she bawled at him, in front of everyone, 'You've just played your last ace, Félix. You may be famous for your lack of talent and your big cock, but to me you're just one more little cunt!'

Félix Marten would add insult to injury and exact his revenge, mere weeks after Piaf's death, by recording a song he claimed to have been inspired by his time with her, 'T'es moche, mais je t'aime' (You're ugly, but I love you). For

Édith, the break-up with Marten initially proved awkward. As her *vedette-américaine*, and under contract for the entire now much-extended Olympia run, she was forced to see him every evening.

Olympia '58 saw Piaf introducing some of the finest songs of her career, though on account of her displeasure with Marten she shelved 'Je me souviens d'une chanson' and left it out of the programme. It was recorded towards the end of the year, and there is an interesting clip of film where she serenades him with it at boulevard Lannes, but it remained elusive during her lifetime. Her subject range was also wider for this series of recitals—from 'Comme moi', which tells the simple story of a woman arranging flowers while waiting for her lover to arrive—to 'Les grognards', which French audiences were able to hear for the first time—to 'Le ballet des coeurs' and 'Mon manège à moi', unusually optimistic numbers by Norbert Glanzberg, who had begun his career writing film scores for Billy Wilder. Later he reflected in the latter, 'The first time Piaf heard it, she said it was shit, but she accepted it just the same.'

> *Tu me fais tourner la tête,*
> *Mon manège à moi, c'est toi!*
> *Je suis toujours à la fête,*
> *Quand tu me prends dans tes bras !*

[You set my head reeling,
You're my very own merry-go-round !
I'm always at the fair,
When you take me in your arms !]

There was also 'La foule', the Spanish song which Piaf had picked up in Peru and had adapted into French by Michel Rivgauche. It is reminiscent of the closing scene in Marcel Carné's famous film, *Les enfants du paradis*, when the mime Baptiste loses his beloved Garance to the hustle-bustle of the carnival throng. In Piaf's version, the bewildered girl finds momentary joy when she is swept into a young man's arms, but her happiness is short-lived when he is just as quickly dragged away from her ...

Je lutte et je me débats et je crispe mes poings,
Maudissant la foule qui me vole
L'homme qu'elle m'avait donné,
Et que je n'ai jamais retrouvé ...

[I fight, struggle and clench my fists,
Cursing the crowd which steals
The man it had given me,
And whom I never found again ...]

No sooner had the curtain fallen on the final recital at the Olympia than Piaf was approached by Marcel Blistène, who since 1946 had been searching for the perfect vehicle to follow *Étoile sans lumière*. In 1948 he had proposed *Macadam*, opposite Marguerite Moreno, but the elderly actress had died while Piaf had been reading the script and the film had been abandoned. Now, she was offered *Les amants de demain*, superbly scripted by an undisputed *monstre sacré* of the French cinema, Pierre Brasseur. It also boasted a fine supporting cast, headed by Michel Auclair, Armand Mestral, Mona Goya in one of her last roles, and Raymond Souplex. But oh, what a woeful tale. Catherine recalled:

> Édith came to see me to ask my advice—whether to do the film, or not. When I saw the script, I told her that this was the kind of story which would have *anyone* reaching for the suicide pills—but that making the film would do her good, and that it would be a great success. The next day she called me. She'd asked Marcel Blistène to give me a part even though I had never acted in my life. And when you watch the film today, you would never believe the riotous time we all had, making it. Every day I came home from the set with my sides aching after listening to Piaf's jokes and anecdotes—most of these about Félix Marten.

The story could have been the setting for one of Piaf's more harrowing songs. Like *Neuf garçons et un Coeur*, it begins one Christmas Eve, though the ensuing events are a far cry from any fantasy. Pierre (Michel Auclair) is a composer, on the run after murdering his cruel wife. His car breaks down and he seeks shelter at Les Géraniums, a provincial guest house which contains the oddest array of characters one can imagine. Here, he is ejected into an even more dreadful situation than the one he has left behind, when he meets Louis, the owner (Armand Mestral), and his drunken, dogsbody wife Simone (Piaf), who for years has been the butt of everyone's jokes and bad moods. The husband is a thug who cheats on her and beats her, hence her addiction to alcohol. Pierre stays the night. He hears Simone singing, and the pair fall in love. Then Louis sees Pierre's photograph in the newspaper, and shops him to the police. There is an argument, he hits Simone once too often, and she shoots him dead. The film ends with the lovers, linked by the death of an abusive and adulterous partner, descending a seemingly endless succession of flights of stairs to the waiting police van—past her husband's spiteful, spitting cronies, whilst Piaf's voice soars over the proceedings singing the title song.

The film's soundtrack was composed by Marguerite Monnot. 'Tant qu'il y aura des jours', which Simone sings whilst in a drunken stupor—and the haunting 'Fais comme si' had lyrics by Michel Rivgauche. Henri Contet wrote the stirring title-track, and the sublime 'Les neiges de Finlande', one of the most poignant lullabies of all time and at just ninety-six seconds, Piaf's shortest song, which Simone sings to her little son:

> *Le Méchant-Loup est un archange,*
> *Les ogres mangent des oranges,*
> *Cendrillon file a laine*
> *Pour habiller l'Croque-Mitaine,*
> *Et je le crois!*
> *Alors je dors sur des légendes,*
> *Et je peux voir dans mon grenier,*
> *Tomber les neiges de Finlande …*

> [The Big Bad Wolf is an archangel,
> Ogres eat oranges,
> Cinderella spins wool to clothe the Bogey-Man,
> And I believe it!
> Thus I sleep on legends, and in my loft I can see
> The falling snows of Finland …]

In France, this song often acts as a 'two minutes' silence' when friends and admirers celebrate Piaf's birthday or the anniversary of her death. More than any of her other songs, it also confirms her childlike belief in fairy tales, superstition and mythology. Catherine explained:

Édith was a female Peter Pan, the little girl who never grew up. On one hand she was worldly and had experienced more in the past few years than most of us would in a dozen lifetimes. On the other she was a naïve child, one who prayed at the foot of her bed, on her knees, and always began by saying, 'Little Jesus, forgive me.' It was this naivety which helped her through the very worst of her problems. She told me she was a poor believer, that she had done more wrong than good in her life. This was untrue. She was a *good* person. The world should never forget this.

In 1958, Piaf published her first autobiography, *Au bal de la chance* (UK: *The Wheel of Fortune*), ghosted and nowhere near as controversial as most people had anticipated. The fabled lovers were all there—Albert the pimp, and the *legionnaire,* who could have been anybody until they were verified in 1963—whilst her relationships with Meurisse, Montand, Jaubert and Contet were kept in a minor key and Cerdan accorded just two paragraphs. Simone Berteaut, and Denise and Herbert Gassion were not mentioned at all, and much of what she wrote about Louis Gassion and Line Marsa was pure invention. The very idea that, having spent so little time together, Piaf had had them buried together in Père Lachaise, was quite frankly laughable. What *is* extremely interesting about the book is Piaf's unpretentious philosophising: she knew precisely what she was writing about because she had *been* there. There is a preface by her friend, Jean Cocteau, who praises her 'Napoleonic forehead' and 'lizardous' hands, and compares her voice with that of the nightingale which toils, hesitates, rasps and chokes, rises and falls before reaching its zenith. He concludes:

> Édith Piaf, like the invisible nightingale installed on her branch, becomes herself invisible. Nothing is left of her but her eyes, her pallid hands, her waxen forehead reflecting the light, and that voice which swells, which mounts, which little by little replaces her. The soul of the street filters into every room of the town. It is no longer Madame Édith Piaf who sings. It is the rain that falls, the wind that blows—the moonlight which spreads its mantle of light.

Au bal de la chance ends with the phrase, 'Better to live than to vegetate,' adopted from another friend, President Eisenhower, someone else who had constantly fought against ill-health. The phrase could just as easily have been Piaf's own. Within days of their showdown in the wings at the Olympia, Félix Marten had been replaced, when her guitarist, Henri Crolla, introduced her to his friend Georges Moustaki. Like others before him, Moustaki forged a pathway to her heart by bringing her a song, 'Le gitan et la fille' the story of the violent young man who tells his girl what will happen to any man who tries to come between them:

> *Le gitan a dit à la fille :*
> *'Qu'importe le prix de l'amour?*
> *Pour toi j'irai finir mes jours derrière les grilles!*
> *J'irai tuer ceux qui te regardent!'*

> [The gypsy told the girl:
> 'Who cares about the price of love?
> For you I'll end my days behind bars!
> I'll kill those who look at you!']

Catherine recalled:

> No sooner was Marten out of her hair than Moustaki came along. Édith was looking for a guitarist for when her regular guitarist Henri Crolla was working elsewhere. Moustaki was not just a guitarist but a singer-songwriter. They met in Édith's dressing-room at the Olympia, and she invited him to her apartment the next day—then when he arrived she refused to see him until he had bathed. The irony is that Moustaki slipped on the wet tiles and dislocated his shoulder, so out of motherly pity, Édith took him in. Henri Crolla was demoted to the position of session musician, and

Moustaki became her personal guitarist, and the new 'boss' at boulevard Lannes. And this one was apparently so special that the cuff-links, tie-pin and cigarette lighter were all made of platinum.

Piaf's life was ruled by superstitions and the spirit world, more so after Marcel Cerdan's death:

> Her friends humoured her because it seemed to be the only way she had of coping with her grief. But there was a big difference between coming to see someone like me, who never took one cent from her, than some of those sitting in on some of the séances she attended ... She told me of how the voice she had heard 'from the beyond' had asked her to make a donation to the Church, and that this should be handed over to her friend [Simone Berteaut] for 'safe keeping'. Édith was so naïve, she did exactly this, and needless to say the money never went to the Church.

Moustaki (1934-2013), was twenty-four when he met Piaf, and four years married with a daughter. Piaf was only made aware of this after he had moved in with her. She *was* suspicious of his intentions, and consulted Catherine, who said she had been aware of Moustaki's violent reputation, but not of his marital status. And, as happened whenever

Piaf asked anyone for advice, she only ever pleased herself. Five years later, she told a reporter from *France Dimanche*:

> This man caused me so much pain that I don't even want to mention his name. He was young, talented, and spirited. I was going through a very lonely phase in my life, and I thought I had found the perfect companion. My astrologer warned me about him, but I took no notice even when I looked at my lover and saw that, in spite of his velvety gaze and tender smile, he was a hard, cynical, dislikeable boy …

After the Olympia, Piaf and Moustaki toured France, with the press having a field-day writing that she was old enough to be his mother. Her reaction to one reporter making this observation was, 'I only wish I was, but then I'd be arrested for incest.' They looked remarkably good together under the spotlight, and on the cover of her EP, *Édith Piaf chante Jo Moustaki*, and she never appeared to 'mother' him in public.

The affair with Moustaki ended badly. In September 1958, Piaf was involved in a car crash at Rambouillet, just outside Paris. Moustaki was driving, with Piaf in the passenger seat, while Marcel Cerdan Jr. and his girlfriend were sitting in the back when the car skidded and somersaulted off the road. While the others suffered only minor injuries, Piaf ended up with a four-inch gash across her forehead, facial abrasions, a split lip, and a severed tendon in her left hand. The car was a total write-off. When one studies the photographs one is amazed that anyone survived at all.

With her already failing health the accident signalled the beginning of the end. Piaf refused to cancel an imminent American tour. Most of her injuries were patched up, but her doctors were worried that the gash on her forehead would leave a scar—unthinkable under the stage lights. She was not bothered about this, and even joked that it would give her more of the 'lived-in' look appropriate for the type of songs she sang. She was however concerned about the split lip, which impeded her speech. Over the next few weeks she subjected herself to a series of agonizing facial massages which put her in such a bad mood that even those closest to her kept their distance. To ease the pain, she began taking morphine again, but this time the dosage was controlled and she did not become addicted.

Piaf flew to New York—with Moustaki by her side, for the time being. On 26 January 1959, instead of the Versailles, she opened in a season at the Waldorf Astoria where she premiered a new Moustaki song, 'Madame La Vierge Marie':

> *Madame la Vierge Marie,*
> *Si j'ai volé, si j'ai mentie,*
> *Pardonnez-moi, je vous en prie,*

J'ai déjà tant et tant souffert,
Ne m'envoyer pas en enfer …

[Madame Virgin Mary,
If I've stolen and lied, I beg you to forgive me,
I've already suffered so much,
Don't send me to hell …]

Piaf entered a New York studio and taped this, and three other Moustaki songs—'Gypsy' (the English version of 'Le gitan et la fille'), 'Faut pas qu'il se figure', and almost certainly an English version of 'Milord'— as will be seen by referring to the discography at the end of this book, the date 24 February listed on the call sheet is an error. In view of what happened next, the songs could only have been recorded prior to 18 February, when she taped two songs for *The Ed Sullivan Show*—'Gypsy', and 'Milord', sung in English and French. Then, two evenings later she was singing 'Heaven Have Mercy', the English adaptation of 'Miséricorde', on stage at the Waldorf Astoria when she collapsed. In her dressing room she vomited blood, and she was rushed to the Presbyterian Hospital on 168th Street, where for four hours a team of surgeons fought to save her life—a perforated stomach ulcer was diagnosed, and she only just managed to pull though. For more than a week, her condition was critical, and fans kept a vigil outside in

Left: The only known picture of Louis Dupont, here with Piaf's first child, Marcelle.

Below left: Piaf wrote 'Hymne à l' amour' in memory of Cerdan, yet had he lived, their affair would not have survived.

Below right: 'En écoutant tinter des muguets'.

Above: 'Find me a new way to die' was always the order of the day where
Michel Emer (L) and Charles Aznavour (R) were concerned.
Looking on and about to be dumped is Eddie Constantine.

Below: 'Cest un homme terrible!' Moustaki gave Piaf some of her finest later songs – and
more than her share of bruises.

Above: Damia, France's greatest singer pre-Piaf

'La belle histoire d'amour'. Piaf in her dressing room,
thirty minutes before the curtain went up on Olympia '61.

Above: Marlene adored and supported Piaf through thick and thin,
but like the rest of her entourage disliked Jacques Pills, the man she married.

Below left: 'The Piaf Gang' at Orly, en route for New York.
Behind her are Ginette Richer and Marc Bonel; *Right:* Reggiani.

Above left: Peggy Lee; *right:* Barbara, France's greatest singer post-Piaf. They shared several songs…and Moustaki.

Below: 'Un enfant est lourde a la fin'. A pregnant Piaf (for the second time) with Simone Berteaut, in Nice, September 1938.

'Mais toi, t'es le dernier!' A radiant Piaf with her Théo, shortly after they wed.

Above: 'Les mômes de la cloche'. Piaf (L) called Simone Berteaut (R) 'my demon spirit', but they were together at every important event in her life. Here they are in Brest, at the time when she was managed by Fernand Lumbroso.

Below: The author in Paris with his godmother, Jacqueline Danno.

the street. Marlene, working in Hollywood, flew across America in the middle of the night just to sit next to her bed. As for Moustaki, he had dumped her and moved on, as she explained in her memoirs:

> When I went into the hospital, I asked him if he loved me. Without even looking at me he said, 'You no longer mean anything to me. Fucking well leave me alone!' I was stunned, and hoped I might die on the operating table. Even so, after my operation I phoned him every day. He'd left me to amuse himself on the beach in Florida. He told me, sarcastically, 'The sun's shining here, and *I'm* in excellent health. There are *girls* here!

Moustaki had replaced Félix Marten overnight. Now, he too received his comeuppance for leaving Piaf in the lurch whilst she had been at death's door. She announced that all of his songs would be removed from her repertoire and for two years, with the exception of 'Milord', was good to her word. On the same day as she recorded this, she recorded 'T'es beau tu sais', the last song Moustaki had written for her. It tells the story of a blind prostitute who reminds her client how beautiful he is by tracing his features with her fingertips—but she never sang this in public. Then in 1961, 'Faut pas qu'il se figure', for which Moustaki had written the music to Michel Rivgauche's lyrics, was 'reprieved' when Piaf asked Charles Dumont to supply a new melody which, it must be said, is superior to the original. Catherine recalled:

> Édith called from the hospital. You can't imagine how much money she spent on transatlantic telephone calls. I thought she would have been more upset over Moustaki than any of the others, because *he* was the one who had left her, and not the other way around. She wasn't. She said that she was happy to be rid of the *salopard*, and that she had already fallen in love again, with [Douglas Davies, of whom more later] a very sexy young American.

For Piaf, meanwhile, life had to go on. After leaving the hospital she returned to the Waldorf Astoria and picked up where she had left off. The Americans had been good to her, she said, and she needed to leave them with happy memories. The huge playbills outside the Empire Room depicted a playing card containing her portrait, above which was the slogan, 'Édith Piaf, Queen of Hearts'. After New York, there was a week-long engagement in Washington: she was paid $40,000 and gave every cent to her entourage who had passed a frugal winter during her illness, accepting work wherever it could be found. Yet when she had offered to pay to send them home to be with their families, not one would leave her.

In the late spring, Piaf embarked on a tour of French-speaking Canada. She had always preferred intimate venues such as Chez Gérard, in Quebec, but Louis Barrier now booked her with the largest halls so as many people could see her as possible. In Montreal, she played the Casino Bellevue, and it was here that she met Claude Leveillé (1932-2011), a young singer-composer who with five friends had recently formed the group, Les Bozos, and opened a small club, La Boîte des Bozos. Piaf turned up here unexpectedly, dozens of her fans followed, and the group was afforded a rapturous standing ovation when they closed their set with 'Les vieux pianos', their attack on 'fake' music:

> *Ce sont vos pianos mécaniques*
> *Que vous avez remplacés par des boîtes à musique,*
> *Qui pour trente sous vous tirent deux disques,*
> *Coup sur coup, pourvu que ça' joue !*
> *Nous on s'en fous!*

> [These are the mechanical pianos
> You have replaced by jukeboxes,
> Which give you two records for thirty sous,
> In rapid succession, provided they play!
> They don't give a fuck about us!]

Piaf asked if she might 'borrow' this, providing she could amend the lyrics slightly. Leveillé agreed. The next day she called him and he was given the official command—she would expect him in Paris, by the end of August at the latest, and with as many songs for her as he could muster, at such short notice. As will be seen, this would cause drama for Piaf's long-suffering entourage. Catherine recalled:

> Within the space of a few weeks, there would be two 'Monsieur Piafs' at boulevard Lannes—and believe me, when things were in full-swing there, one was more than enough to deal with. For a little while, I kept my distance, though Édith and I did speak on the phone most days …

Catherine was witness to the 'circus' which took place at boulevard Lannes while Piaf was preparing for Olympia '61. The premiere had been set for 29 December 1960, but came close to being cancelled when Piaf confided in Bruno Coquatrix that a clairvoyant—*not* Catherine—had predicted that she would die on stage. Then on Christmas Day, while rehearsing at a cinema in Versailles, she received a telegram from Marlene Dietrich, wishing her luck, and dismissed the prediction as 'bunkum'. Marlene was about to take on the most foreboding challenge of her later career— her first visit in thirty years to the Germany she had turned her back on, on account of the stance the country of her birth had taken during the war. This telegram dispelled any suggestion that Édith's friend had deserted her in her hour of need. Now, the show could go on, as Catherine recalled:

> Boulevard Lannes was just like a mad-house. Well-wishers filed in and out all day, most of whom were not sure whether they were helping Piaf prepare for a comeback, or encouraging her towards an early grave. Her new black dress and shoes arrived first thing, but at the last moment she changed her mind and wore an old pair of slip-ons and a dress she had been singing in for years. The stench of camphor was overpowering, but she declared that to wear anything else would have been unlucky. And I don't think I had ever seen her looking so radiant. She was literally dying on her feet, yet she'd managed to convince herself that she was invincible. We knew that it wouldn't last, but all that mattered was seeing her happy—*truly* happy for the first time in years.

14: Charles Dumont

■   ■   ■

During the autumn of 1960, a very sick Piaf began rehearsing for a fifteen-venue tour of the provinces, to be followed by a season at the Paris Olympia which would turn out to be the greatest triumph of her entire career. This was sheer madness, her entourage declared, and became known as the 'suicide tour'. Since collapsing onstage in America, and almost dying on the operating table, there had been several relapses and there would be others during the tour. Her doctors had warned her time and time again that she was slowly killing herself, yet she refused to yield. Singing was her life—if she stopped singing, she said, life would have no meaning and she might as *well* be dead. Her friends, even her musicians who relied on her for their income, begged her not to do the tour, and to just focus her attention on the Olympia recitals. And then, a miracle happened. On 5 October 1960, her lyricist friend Michel Vaucaire brought about a meeting with a thirty-one-year-old composer who would not only help resurrect Piaf's self-confidence, he would inadvertently offer her three more years of life.

His name was Charles Dumont, and he had composed hits for Tino Rossi, Dalida and Cora Vaucaire, Michel's wife and one of France's best-loved singers. Piaf, for reasons unknown, had always refused to have anything to do with him. In 1990, he recalled their first 'encounter':

> I was invited into her vast, cluttered living room. Before leaving home I received a telegram saying that she was too ill to see me, but assuming this was just another of her excuses, I pretended not to have seen it. She yelled out from another room that seeing as I was there, she might as well see me, and said she would be out in a minute. Then she kept me standing there for over an hour—I wasn't even offered a chair. When Piaf came into the room, she looked a fright—she was wearing a nightdress several sizes too big for her, odd carpet slippers, and she hardly had any hair. And she was *so* rude, telling me to play my song and get it over with, and then clear off.

Simone Berteaut claimed that Piaf had told her that she had initially disliked Dumont, adding, 'He was dressed like a civil servant, and couldn't stop staring at his shoes. If he'd have been a travelling salesman he wouldn't have made a single sale, even with God on his side.'

Feeling decidedly ill at ease, Charles sat at Édith's piano. The music he had composed, to a lyric by Michel Vaucaire, was 'Non, je ne regrette rien', and the rest is an essential part of the Piaf legend. Charles recalled:

> She had stood hunched over the piano, her head on one side and not looking very pleased, and as I finished the song I was expecting her to bring the lid down on my fingers. Then she straightened up and asked, 'Did you *really* write that?' When I nodded, she cried, 'But it's *wonderful!*'—and as if by magic all the lines of illness seemed to drop off her face, and her attitude towards me changed alarmingly. *Then* it was as if we'd been friends her whole life.

Dumont and Vaucaire had actually written the song back in 1956, but with different lyrics (as had happened with their 'Mon Dieu', which had started off as 'Toulon-Le Havre-Anvers'). 'Non, je ne regrette rien' would give Piaf her biggest international hit—she also recorded it in English, and would have done so in German and Italian, had this not been prevented by illness. The song would be adopted by the French Foreign Legion, at that time involved in the Algerian War, as their unofficial anthem:

Non, rien de rien!
Non, je ne regrette rien!
Ni le bien qu'on m'a fait,
Ni le mal!
Tout ça m'est bien égal!

[Nothing whatsoever!
No, I regret nothing!
Neither the good nor the bad done to me!
It's all the same to me!]

By the end of 1960, Charles Dumont would be regarded as Piaf's principal composer, replacing even the stalwart Marguerite Monnot. Eleven Monnot songs were to be performed at the Olympia, including 'C'est l'amour', for which Piaf had written the words, and which would be used to close the show. She had recorded this on 13 May for her *Huit chansons nouvelles* album (Columbia FS1083), a work of such professionalism that every song had been recorded with a single take, enabling the album to be released within one week. 'T'es beau tu sais', 'Ouragan' and 'Le vieux piano' have already been mentioned. Julien Bouquet's 'Je suis à toi' was a surreal study of lost love:

Once, the springtime repainted the grey walls of Paris,
and this reflected in the lovers' eyes …
but now those days are gone,

and life will ever be grey unless you return and tell me,
'I am yours!'

Robert Gall's and Florence Véran's 'Les amants merveilleux'
tells of the lovers who pass by in a deserted street, eyes half-
closed and oblivious to the world ... the narrator is afraid
of witnessing such happiness until she runs into the arms
of her lover and realizes how lucky she is. 'Cri de coeur', a
poem by Jacques Prévert set to music by Henri Crolla, was
a rare, self-indulgent study of Piaf *by* Piaf: without pity she
has walked over her tears and never made them public, and
if the landscape was too ugly, she merely waited for beauty
to reappear ... and though she has hardly ever seen love's
face, should she meet it again she will recognize it all the
same. An oddment—in that it was not a new song but from
the November 1957 session which had produced 'La foule',
was 'Opinion publique', a complex work and a *chanson-
parlée*. Wherever he goes, the man is pursued by rumour—
in the street, in cafés and bars. His reputation is advertised
all over town—until one day he stands up in the market
place and yells, 'It's not true.' Now, he is a famous man,
but the rumours are the same. C'est l'amour', however, rises
high above its contemporaries, even on such a very eclectic
album, and what makes it even more poignant is that it was
the very last Marguerite Monnot song she recorded. Piaf
told a British reporter who witnessed the recording process,

'I know all there is to know about love—and I also know
how much it costs.'

> *Dans l'amour il faut des larmes,*
> *Dans l'amour il faut donner ...*
> *Et ceux qui n'ont pas de larmes,*
> *Ne pourront jamais aimer!*
> *J'ai pleuré pour mieux t'aimer,*
> *J'ai payé de tant de larmes,*
> *Pour toujours le droit d'aimer!*

> [In love there must be tears ... and giving,
> And the ones who don't have tears may never love!
> I've cried, to better love you,
> I've paid with so many tears,
> For the eternal right to love!]

This and nine of the other Monnot songs were dropped
from the Olympia programme to make way for Dumont
songs. The only 'survivor' was 'Les blouses blanches', which
would close the Olympia concert but never be recorded in
the studio. Without any doubt it is the most disturbing song
Piaf ever sang—it had far-reaching effects on one member
of the audience, who collapsed in the auditorium and had
to be stretchered out, resulting in it being removed from
Piaf's repertoire. The 'white-coats' are the warders in the
lunatic asylum ... She's been locked up with the lunatics for

eight years. It's because of the white-coats that she's there. They keep telling her she's not mad. She remembers a white dress she once had, a pretty dress with flowers. Then, a hand held hers, a beautiful hand with fingers which sang. But she isn't mad. She'll go on loving—forever.

Some believed that Piaf's 'desertion' of Monnot— who until now had been her very best friend—took away Monnot's will to live. She and Piaf had been by far the most successful female song-writing team in Europe, and when Monnot developed appendicitis during the summer of 1961, declaring that she had nothing left to live for, she refused to have treatment. She died of peritonitis on 12 October 1961, almost two years to the day before Piaf, who is said to have never forgiven herself for treating the 'woman' of her life the way she had most of her men.

In all, Dumont wrote the music for thirty Piaf songs, almost all of them million-sellers during her lifetime. The tables were turned, so to speak, when Piaf wrote a song for *him*, 'La fille qui pleurait dans la rue', and they recorded duets—'Les amants', which set Dumont on the path towards an immensely successful singing career of his own, and 'Inconnu excepté de Dieu', where the subject is not a person, but a grave discovered while walking past a meadow:

Quel destin à vrai dire, repose sous ce granit bleu ?
Est-ce un enfant, ou est-ce un homme,
Pour qui la mort fit, c'est tant mieux?
Deux mètres carré de royaume …
'Inconnu excepte de Dieu'.

[What fate, indeed, rests beneath this blue granite?
Is it a child, or is it a man
For whom death was so much the better?
A two-metres-square kingdom …
'Unknown, except by God!']

15: Barbara

■　　　■　　　■

Barbara (1930-97) remains France's greatest singer after Piaf—indeed, some critics and students of the *chanson* who believed that, towards the end of her life, the lady born Monique Serf actually surpassed her, particularly with a regard to her humanist work. For almost twenty years, she was one of my closest friends. I adapted several of her songs into English for her, and wrote one especially for her. No one inspired me more than Barbara did.

Barbara confessed to attending every one of Piaf's Olympia premieres, but only met her twice—the second meeting but a chance encounter—but they are linked by songs they shared: 'A l'enseigne de la fille sans coeur', 'Quand tu dors', 'Un monsieur me suit dans la rue', and 'La petite boutique' a rarely heard gem by Roméo Carlés, written in the wake of the Leplée scandal in 1936:

> *Quand je suis trop affectée par les potins …*
> *Par scandales dégoûtants, des requins de la politique,*
> *Afin de mieux m'éloigner d'eux,*
> *Je vais passer une heure ou deux*
> *Dans cette petite boutique …*

[When I'm too affected by gossips,
By disgusting scandals and political sharks,
To better get away from them,
I go and spend an hour or two in this little shop …]

There was also 'C'est un homme terrible'. It tells of the man who uses his woman as 'target practice' with his fists, who makes her tremble with fear when he is late home, and who both terrifies and crucifies her—yet when night comes, *he* is the one afraid of the dark, whilst *she* is the strong one—until morning comes and he returns to being his cruel self.

Jean-Pierre Moulin wrote the song for Piaf in 1958 after she had recounted her 'experiences' with Georges Moustaki. So that he would not think she was referring to him, Édith insisted to Moulin that the narrative be changed to the third person, though it is obvious who she is referring to.

During the late-Sixties, Barbara was also involved with Moustaki. They had a huge success in France with a duet, 'La dame brune', though reflecting on him did not bring back very happy memories and confirmed stories told by others of Édith's fondness for men who were mean, moody and violent:

Moustaki's bohemian spirit was very much like Piaf's own, so her unusual lifestyle—living in an apartment she had never really moved into, surrounded by boxes and crates all the time—never put him off. Moustaki never minded slaving over the same song for hours on end. He tolerated the snatched meals and cat-naps because, he claimed, he was a gypsy at heart. But despite his immense, immense talent, he was not always an agreeable man, and he had a very nasty, unpredictable streak.

Édith's favourite female singer was always Marie Dubas (1894-1972). She very rarely spoke about her closest rivals, Damia and Fréhel, but always had a tremendous respect and admiration for the woman she called 'La Grande Marie', who had retired in 1955 owing to failing health. In the late 1950s, as 78 rpm records gave way to vinyl and many of the great retro stars were enjoying a revival with the re-release of their material, because she had committed but a fraction of her sizeable repertoire to shellac, Marie was overlooked. Enter Barbara, starting to make a name for herself having just been awarded the Grand Prix du Disque for her interpretations of Georges Brassens:

> At the end of 1960, I learned that Marie was ill and suffering from depression, convinced that after her years at the top of the showbusiness ladder, she had now been completely forgotten. I decided to do something about this, and as a result of a campaign

launched by myself and a few friends, I was able to visit Marie's apartment and present her with over four thousand letters of admiration and support from her fans. The next day, I received a call from Piaf. She expressed no desire to meet me, though I did eventually go to boulevard Lannes—all she wanted was for me to help her compose a letter of complaint to Pathé-Marconi. When she called me again she told me what she'd told the director over the phone, 'Marie made a fortune for you during her hey-day. What gratitude do you show her now that she's ill? Get off your backside and do something about it, otherwise Piaf is going to be leaving Pathé-Marconi.' He listened, because he knew that without Piaf, the company would have lost a fortune. They released an album of Marie Dubas songs. It sold thousands of copies, and this introduced her to a new generation of fans. More than this, her type of song—not the réaliste songs, but the spoofs and comedy numbers she had performed so well, started to come back into fashion.

Barbara's second meeting with Piaf took place during the afternoon of 3 December 1962, at the Pathé-Marconi studios. Édith was there to record 'Le rendez-vous', by Francis Lai and René Rouzaud—her very last studio recording which was laid down in a single take. Barbara, who since last seeing her had enjoyed considerable success this time with an album of songs by Jacques Brel, watched this final session through a security window. She recalled:

> I had just taken to performing my own songs, and was at the studio to rehearse 'Chapeau-bas' in the very next room, the one and only time our names appeared on the same bill—in this instance, in chalk on the blackboard inside the foyer. I was excited because I was hoping to arrange another visit to see Marie Dubas, and was sure that this time, Piaf would come with me. Like a fragile little black bird, but still with an immensely powerful voice, she sang her song. Then she collapsed into a heap. My heart skipped a beat. I was sure she was dead, the way she hit the floor. Then her husband [Théo Sarapo] gathered her up in his arms like a bundle of rags and carried her to the car. I held the door open as they passed through, and that's the nearest I ever got to meeting her again. And you ask which of Piaf's songs was my favourite? Well, there are so many to choose from, but I guess for nostalgic reasons it would have to be the one by Lechanois.

Barbara was referring to 'Un monsieur me suit dans la rue', which Piaf had recorded in January 1944:

Quand on m'a suivie dans la rue,
Ce n'était qu'un vieux dégoûtant ...

Je sais qu'on le poursuit,
Pour le mettre en prison.

[When he followed me in the street,
He was just a dirty old man …
I knew someone was following him,
To put him in prison …]

Not the kind of song one might hear on the radio today, this tells of the little girl—she makes a point of stressing this by saying that she still plays with toys—who is followed home by a child molester. Yet she does not want him to be arrested by the police, and when he catches up with her and invites her back to his place, she submits willingly because even being with him will be better than going home. The song ends with the child falling ill and expressing her greatest wish—to be finally shown affection and respect, by stopping the traffic and having decent people following her through the street at her funeral. Barbara had closed her act with it when making her debuts at L'Écluse, the little cabaret on the Left Bank, in the late Fifties:

> I identified very much with that song because my
> own childhood was not always happy. I closed my
> show with it, in the hope that each time I did this,
> I was closing just a little more that part of my life
> that I so wanted to forget.

16: Roger Normand

■　　■　　■

My godfather started out during World War II as one of
Mistinguett's dancers. In 1950, he branched out on his own
as a singer-songwriter—Charles Dumont was his pianist,
for a time. Roger and Piaf first met in 1946, just after she
had finished working on *Étoile sans lumière*, and in 1954
he approached her with a song, 'Gueule d'ange', which he
had written for the soundtrack of the film of the same name
which he had also scripted. Édith dismissed the song as 'too
syrupy', and he gave it to Dany Dauberson, a popular singer
of the day who had a big hit with it:

> Édith called me and asked me to bring her a copy
> of the record so that she could listen to it—I don't
> know why, because they were playing it on the
> radio all the time. She smashed it over the edge
> of the table, and told me never to mention 'that
> fucking woman' ever again in her presence. But we
> remained friends.

Piaf and Roger also shared several lovers, which never
caused any friction between them:

Sometimes I ended up with the cast-offs when she or Miss or somebody else had worn them out, such as Toto Gérardin, who was a total wreck when we'd all finished with him. Occasionally I would introduce her to a new boyfriend, and she would steal him off me—though she always returned him in one piece.

Like Marlene, Roger advised Piaf against getting involved with Jacques Pills—and like Marlene he had also taken an instant aversion towards Georges Moustaki:

Édith was one of those women who genuinely believed that to get to a man's heart, you had to feel the force of his fist. During the years that I knew her, I saw her with some real shiners. She confided in me, 'He beats the shit out of me, but when he's asleep in my arms; it's like nursing a child. Isn't it wonderful? Now I know that I've got a man who *really* loves me.' And it's true. During her 'Greek summer', as she called it, she was happier than I'd seen her in years.

Roger recalled Piaf's almost manic possessiveness and jealousy, should the man in her life—be he lover or composer—not afford her his undivided attention. Henri Contet, Marcel Cerdan, Eddie Constantine, Toto Gérardin, Félix Marten and Moustaki had all been married, and apparently happily so, but such had been the lure of success which being involved with her had guaranteed, that Piaf had taken advantage of the situation with demands so extraneous that some of their marriages had collapsed. One of her failures in this respect had been Charles Dumont:

> There was always a certain amount of distance between them, even though they were hardly ever apart. With no regular man in her life—indeed she was so preoccupied with what she called her resurrection that she only had time for her work—Édith was more ruthless than ever. She kept Dumont away from his wife and daughters, then tried to convince everyone that *he* was ashamed of being with them because he had something to hide, which of course was not true. She gushed all over him every minute he was in the room, yet he only had to be out of it for five minutes and she'd yell, 'Where's Dumont? Why has he walked out?' One of us would say, 'But Édith, he's only in the bathroom.' Then she would bawl, 'The bathroom, be damned. The sneaky bastard's on the phone to [Lucienne] Delyle, or Patachou. Those two bitches have spent their entire careers stealing other people's songs.' Then Charles would come back into the room, and she'd fuss all over him again. But before Dumont, there were Leveillé and Douglas Davies. My God, I don't think she had any plates left after those two.

Douglas Davies was a twenty-three-year-old painter from Atlanta, Georgia, who during a trip to New York had gone to see Piaf at the Waldorf Astoria, hoping to meet her and pluck up the courage to ask her to sit for him. Instead, he had seen her collapse on the stage. During her illness he had visited the hospital every day, and rather than buy her huge bouquets like other fans, he had brought simple bunches of violets, unaware of her foibles and superstitions. This, and the fact that he spent two hours every day on the New York subway bringing them to her, touched her. Later, she wrote:

> Faced with Doug's naïve expression and cordial smile, I knew that I'd been given the will to live again. One afternoon he brought me five gaily coloured balloons. He gave them to me because I had told him that balloons had been my childhood dream, and that my father had never wanted to buy me any. Then I kissed him for the first time ...

The American media did not approve of Piaf and Doug's affair. Many people considered him far too young for her, and an opportunist. Doug accompanied her to Washington and Canada, not leaving her side for one moment—while she was on stage, he was standing in the wings.

Douglas Davies had unexpectedly replaced Moustaki in Piaf's affections. It had mattered little to her that he was bisexual and that he also had an American boyfriend—he was by no means the only one of her lovers to 'swing both ways'. Returning to Paris on 21 June 1959, she took him with her. Newsreel footage shows her being lifted from the steps of the plane by Bruno Coquatrix, then gradually being swallowed up by the loving arms of her friends, whilst Doug is being pushed more and more into the crowd of journalists and reporters. Then, as if suddenly remembering that she had left something behind on the plane, she turns around to search for him in the sea of faces. Eventually he is introduced to everyone and she announces, in English, 'You must remember how to pronounce his name—not Davis, but *Davies!*' Throughout their brief but eventful relationship she would never miss out on the opportunity to rebuke anyone who mispronounced his name—yet in her memoirs, *she* calls him *Davis*.

Piaf would never forget her debt of gratitude towards Doug Davies and despite some of their very public differences of opinion, from now on there would be few photographs or newsreel clips of her where she does not look gloriously happy. At boulevard Lannes another welcoming committee was headed by Marguerite Monnot and Georges Moustaki—he had returned to France ahead of her and was still living at the apartment, obviously expecting to be forgiven and welcomed back into the fold. This was filmed to be shown on the television news that night. When the group gathered around the piano to sing 'Milord'—the first time anyone in France had heard the song—Piaf pushed them laughingly aside, told them how they were ruining it by singing off-key, and sang it herself. Throughout, Doug skulked around out of camera, levelling obscene remarks at the man he only ever referred to as 'that Greek motherfucker'. And once the television crew and Monnot left, there were fireworks when the two men almost ended up brawling because Piaf had told Doug of how Moustaki had liked knocking her around. Moustaki left in a huff—a great pity in terms of her repertoire, for there would be no more songs of the calibre of 'Milord' and 'Eden Blues'.

In Paris, propelled into the chaos of Piaf's bohemian existence, Doug was out of his depth. He was an artist, albeit not a well-known one, and he was in the cultural centre of his world with galleries and museums waiting to be explored. Typically tyrannical, Piaf refused to let him out of her sight, and also had the habit of having the central-heating on full power, distressing for everyone in the middle of June. She contacted Catherine Jan and asked her to come to boulevard Lannes and sit in on a séance—she needed to contact Marcel Cerdan and gain his approval of her new lover. Catherine was out of town therefore Piaf took Doug to see a clairvoyant who scared the life out of the young man by announcing that he and Piaf would soon be dead. Tragically, he was not wrong.

In August 1959, there was more drama when Claude Leveillé arrived in Paris, and naturally he moved straight into Piaf's apartment, ruffling Doug Davies' feathers. Over the next few weeks, she played one off against the other. Doug was let off his leash and allowed to visit some of the galleries—Piaf accompanied him, though she knew very little about art, whilst Leveillé was placed under 'house arrest', as had happened with Michel Émer the first time he had visited New York, and ordered to stay put until he had written her a song. Within days he had collaborated with Michel Rivgauche on 'Boulevard du Crime', in every sense a miniature symphony which Leveillé himself sang exceedingly well in his Brel-like tones a few years later:

> Sur le boulevard de Crime, pour voir la pantomime
> Ce soir on se bouscule au Théâtre des Funambules.
> Masques sans bergamasques
> Pour les danses fantasques, et,
> La foule coasse au milieu du Carnival des Grimaces.

> [On the Boulevard of Crime, to see the pantomime,
> Tonight they jostle at the Funambules.
> Mummers without masks for whimsical dances,

And the crowd croaks in the middle
Of the Carnival of Grimaces ...]

Leveillé is believed to have based what many regard as his greatest work on the real-life 'carnival' chez Piaf. If so, his study was an accurate one. He wrote around a dozen songs for her, but because of the ups and downs in her health and private life—and with the advent of Charles Dumont—besides 'Boulevard du Crime' she recorded only 'Ouragan' and 'Les vieux pianos'. The others never progressed beyond the acetate or tape-recording stage. As for 'Les vieux pianos', this caused considerable ill-feeling between Piaf and Leveillé when he learned that she had handed his song over to Henri Contet, without acquiring his permission, and asked him to rewrite the lyric so that only two of its original lines remained, and the work was retitled 'Le vieux piano'. Roger Normand recalled:

> Leveillé accused her of sacrilege, but I don't supposed he complained about all the royalties. Then the shit really hit the fan when she found out that he had 'done a Moustaki' on her—that he had a wife back home that he'd conveniently forgotten to mention. Then there was another bust-up with Doug Davies when he found out that Piaf had only been keeping him hanging on until she'd ensnared Leveillé. Effectively, she ended up losing them

both, though I don't think there was ever anything physical between her and Leveillé.

The news of Leveillé's marriage reached Piaf's ears by way of a telephone call—taken by Mômone, who for once was not acting in her own interest—from his father, informing him that his wife had given birth to a son. The marriage ended soon afterwards, and few years later the little boy died. Piaf, meanwhile, was about to embark on a provincial tour, and she made it clear that she was not expecting Leveillé to still be there when she came back to Paris. He eventually returned to Montréal, where he opened his own club, Le Chat Noir. From a distance, he and Piaf would remain friends and he would compose for her again in the not too distant future.

Because Doug Davies disliked driving 'foreign' cars, Piaf bought him an expensive, customized Chevrolet. He was driving on the first day of the tour when it shot off the road, near Divone, and crashed into a barrier. Doug was unhurt, but Piaf, sitting in the rear, broke three ribs. There was no question of cancelling, and in order to sing that night she was given a single morphine injection. This reacted with the cortisone she had been prescribed for her rheumatism which had been getting worse—so much so that at times she could hardly manipulate her hands. The cortisone bloated her features. On the stage, audiences saw a pathetic little Piaf doll in a black dress, her make-up smudged and her stockings creased. Only the Piaf voice had changed for the better. While recovering she allowed Doug to paint her portrait—this later appeared on the cover of the *Olympia '61* album, and a subsequent portrait would appear on the cover of her *C'est l'amour* EP.

During a break in the tour, Piaf and Doug spent a short time in Cannes, where they rented a suite at the Hôtel Majestic. They argued one day when he turned out wearing just a pair of swimming shorts, for Piaf was jealous of the other women on the beach admiring his fine, athletic body. He placated her somewhat by buying her a modest swimming costume, and giving her lessons. Such was Piaf's naivety that she broke her own cast-iron 'late-to-bed-late-to-rise' sleeping rule and rose at dawn every morning to suffer an agonizing hour in the sea, just to watch the other bathers' faces, since her presence always drew a sizeable crowd. She even wrote a song about this brief period, 'T'es l'homme qu'il me faut', which Charles Dumont later set to music:

> *Quand j'sors avec toi, j'm'accroche à ton bras,*
> *Les femmes, elle te voient,*
> *Toi, tu n'les vois pas, heureusement pour moi!*
> *T'es l'homme qu'il me faut!*

[When I go out with you, I hang on to your arm,
Women see you,
But happily for me you don't see them!
You're the man for me!]

Cannes offered Doug a once-in-a-lifetime chance to meet his idol, Picasso, a meeting arranged by Piaf—and which in turn led to him meeting Virgil Thomson, Piaf's old ally who in turn inducted him into the coterie of 'exiled' Riviera American homosexuals headed by the concert pianist, Ned Rorem. Roger continued the story:

> In Cannes, Duggie was happy to be amongst his own kind—and by that I mean the intellectual set. He had admired Picasso his whole life, and now he could finally meet him. Piaf tried to hang on to him. She even bought a costume and talked him into teaching her how to swim. Then they had an almighty row and she flung a teapot at him. Duggie slapped her—for her, the ultimate proof of his love—but instead of taking her to bed, as the others had, he walked out in the middle of the night and caught the train back to Paris. Charles Dumont and Michel Vaucaire turned the incident into a song …

This was 'C'est peut-être ça', which sees the woman waiting for the telephone call that never comes—and who rushes out into the pouring rain at midnight, screaming that the weather is fine, while in pursuit of the man who has walked out on her.

Ever the Svengali, Piaf had been responsible for launching or boosting the careers of so many of her lovers—Montand, Moustaki, Meurisse and Jaubert, Asso, Carlés, Contet. Her only failures were Félix Marten and a strange young man named Claude Figus. Roger explained:

> Édith had known Figus for years. Today you would call him a groupie. He was twenty-one or so when he met her backstage at the Olympia in 1955 and was absolutely obsessed by her, though not in a dangerous way. He wasn't all that handsome, though I guess he must have been good between the sheets. He was sweet as sugar, but an absolute creep. He was working as a rent-boy when they met, and she fell for his charm and asked him to be her secretary, and even then he was still plying his trade—picking up men in the Bois de Boulogne, just across from Piaf's apartment. You should have seen some of the monuments he took back to boulevard Lannes. Even *she* was shocked.

Figus may have been Piaf's most devoted servant, but he was also her biggest liability. During the worst part of her alcoholism he had helped her hide bottles all over the apartment, and had always refused to take part in the 'booze-searches' organized by her friends. Worse than this, he would wait until the household was asleep, then sneak her out to an all-night bar or club. He had begun his 'career' as a rent-boy at fourteen, but appears to have also sold his charms to women, and even boasted that he had enjoyed a brief spell as Piaf's lover during the darkest days of her addictions. He did spend a lot of time with her at the clinic, and on neutral territory his presence was certainly more beneficial than that of Jacques Pills, who was only interested in Piaf's money. When Olympia '61 closed on 13 April and she embarked on another tour he never left her side for a moment, and he made such a fuss when she collapsed on 25 May, insisting that instead of wasting time waiting for an ambulance, he and Louis Barrier should drive her to hospital. Here, an emergency operation was carried out for intestinal adhesions, and there is no doubting that his 'fussing' saved her life. Figus was with her much of the time when she elected to dictate her memoirs, as Roger explained:

> Édith had written her 'life story' before, and was the first to admit that what she'd written in *Au bal de la chance* had been tamed down. The Piaf in that book was not the Piaf we'd known and loved for years. One afternoon, Hughes Vassal came to see her—he

was a photographer with *France Dimanche*, and one
of the few she trusted not to take pictures of her that
made her look bad. Vassal brought a reporter called
Jean Noli with him. Édith took to him when she let
something slip which would normally have made
the headlines, but which Noli kept to himself. In
next to no time, she'd decided that if she *was* going
to tell the real Piaf story, it would be to him. She
told me, 'Noli belongs to a rare breed of journalist,
one with a heart and conscience.'

Piaf opened her heart to Jean Noli—something she had
rarely done with any man. Her recollections were listed
under tabloid-type headings—'*My Man, My Men!*', '*I'm
Unfaithful!*', '*I Drank To Forget!*'—not published in *France
Dimanche*, but assembled by Noli to form her second
autobiography, *Ma vie*, published in 1963. Astonishingly,
the book did not cause that much of a stir. Because much
of Noli's information had been collated between bouts
of ill-health and hospitalizations, sceptics doubted its
authenticity: not just how much of it was the result of Piaf's
overworked imagination while obviously on medication,
but how much had been fabricated by the editor. On more
careful inspection, with the passing of time and so many of
those connected to Piaf at the time now dead—the entire
script would appear to be genuine. Only a few names have

been changed, or in the case of Gérardin and Moustaki omitted entirely. Roger concluded:

Édith was dying, and she was well aware of this. She wanted to get it all off her chest before it was too late. As for Figus, I've already said that he was a creep, because he had eyes everywhere and reported everything back to her like some kind of spy. He was forever pitching one of us against the other—and of course Édith herself loved nothing more than to see us all arguing and at each other's throats. But to his credit he was no opportunist. No one at boulevard Lannes ever saw Figus ask Édith for money. I saw her *offer* him money, and I also saw him refuse it, saying that he didn't want to be thought of as a leech, like the others. I guess he helped himself to other things, though the participants were always willing. When Édith brought Doug Davies back from America, it didn't take Figus long to seduce him. And yet, whenever she was ill—which was often in those days—he slept on the floor next to her bed like a faithful little puppy. Then at around the time of Olympia '61 she launched his singing career with a song called 'Quand l'amour est fini'. The record flopped. Then he got arrested by the police—he'd been out, got drunk, and decided to fry eggs for Édith's breakfast over the eternal flame at the Arc de Triomphe. She found the episode hilarious and paid his fine. And then, in January 1962, everything changed …

Through wealthy clients involved with the cinema, Figus had been given bit-parts in three films (*La nuit des traqués, Les dragueurs, Pêcheur d'Islande*), and showed promise as an actor. This changed when Piaf heard him sing, for he really did have a good voice. After securing him a contract with Polydor, she supervised his first session with the studio in 1961, and arranged another for the spring of 1962. His 'Les enfants de la terre', set to Albinoni's *Adagio*, is especially moving. 'A t'aimer comme j'ai fait', was dedicated to his new lover: Théophanis Lamboukas, a strapping, inordinately handsome twenty-six-year-old Parisian-born hairdresser of Greek heritage, whom Piaf virtually ignored the first time Figus took him home. This changed a few weeks later when she was rushed into the Ambroise Paré Clinic, in Neuilly, suffering from double bronchial pneumonia:

> After their first meeting, she'd dismissed [Théo] as a 'brooding little shirt-lifter'. The first time I saw him, he was perched on the edge of the sofa, twiddling his thumbs and seemingly lost for words—hardly surprising, when one considers Piaf's powerful aura, and her insistence that all visitors to her court be spirited and cheerful, which she certainly *always* was, no matter how lousy she felt. Theo was a

polite, well-spoken young man, and that got up her nose a bit. She went out of her way to be unpleasant and vulgar, going on about what men 'like him' did in bed with each other. And Théo just sat there, smiling. Then, when Édith was ill, he accompanied Figus to the clinic, until one morning when he and Figus had a row, and he went alone. All her other friends took her huge bouquets of flowers, but Théo took her a bunch of daisies and a Greek doll. That did it, of course.

Two of Piaf's former lovers had been Greek—Moustaki, and Takis Menelaus. Therefore with her penchant for superstition, she regarded Théo as a 'third-time-lucky' omen. There were no tantrums, and no jealousy, where the last man in Édith's life was concerned. Finding his name too difficult to pronounce, she re-baptized him Théo Sarapo— from *s'agapo*, the Greek for 'I love you.' He asked her if he might set her hair—not knowing how sensitive she was about the fact that she hardly had any hair left. She agreed, and promptly fell in love with him, aware that he and Claude Figus were still an on-off item, and therefore almost certainly aware of how he had once earned a living:

They were still sleeping together, even after Théo had become the new 'Monsieur Piaf'. Figus considered it his divine right because *he'd* brought them together in the first place, and even Édith maintained, initially at least until they became very serious about each other, that sharing Théo was better than not having him at all. She called me one day and chirped, 'Théo and I both have the same taste in men—the stiffer the better!'

Inasmuch as Piaf performed so many songs where the subjects had been female prostitutes, so she appears to have been fascinated by rent-boys, as Roger explained:

> Claude Figus was a rent-boy until the day he died, and Théo had worked as one too, when younger. Piaf knew this, and this is how 'Monsieur Incognito' came about. The audience knew nothing about the story behind the song, which was Piaf's and Théo's secret little joke.

The song, with which Piaf would audaciously open her joint recitals with Théo—her very last—in February 1963 at the Bobino, was written by Florence Véran and Robert Gall. It tells the story of the male prostitute who works his beat outside her Métro station. With his fine clothes, well-shined shoes, and sophisticated disposition others might mistake him for just another passer-by, but *she* knows what he is up to, and instinctively hates him because when she was lonely, and feeling miserable, there were never such men on the street to comfort *her*. Therefore all she can do is scream at him, '*Go away!*'

Even more curious were the songs in Théo's early repertoire, all written by Piaf, about youngsters who come to a sticky end. In 'Chez Sabine' there are echoes of 'L'homme à la moto' with the twenty-year-old know-it-all who shows off to his girlfriend by speeding in his flashy Jaguar, only to end up killing them both. In the clamorous 'La bande en noir'—the true story of a drug-runner friend of Claude Figus who had recently received his comeuppance from another thug he had wronged in the past, the outcome is equally grim:

> *Pas une fille ne l'intéresse …*
> *Tout une jeunesse de foutue,*
> *Et ses vingt ans qu'il a perdu,*
> *Étendu là sur le trottoir c'était pas joli à voir!*

> [Not one girl interested him …
> A youth, entirely fucked up,
> And his twenty years which he lost, there,
> Stretched out on the pavement, not a pretty sight!]

Theirs certainly was a bizarre relationship: a gay man and a woman who virtually had one foot in the grave. Yet as a partner, Théo was more devoted towards caring about

Piaf's welfare, and with little thought for himself, than *any* predecessor, period. On bad days, he cut up her food and spoon-fed her. He spent hours reading to her: she was deeply into the classics and adored André Gide and others of his [French Symbolist] genre. He shared with Piaf something he had never shared with his family—his horrendous experiences when he had spent his entire two-year military service at Colomb-Bechar, a remote outpost in Algeria, where he had lost thirty pounds in weight, and where his only comfort had come from listening to Piaf's recordings on his portable record-player. And when he told her one day that his dream had always been to sing, Édith's own recovery was nothing short of miraculous. Now she had something to live for. From now on, wherever she performed, there was no question of Théo *not* being her *vedette-américaine*.

Neither was Théo the 'timid and gentle lamb' everyone perceived him to be, particularly if he suspected someone from 'the Piaf circus' of trying to extort money from her—or if someone was not treating her with the respect she deserved. A particular thorn in his side were the 'siblings' who kept turning up: Mômone, aka Simone Berteaut, who claimed to have been Piaf's sister, and who she referred to as her 'demon spirit', but never made any effort to get rid of her—and Herbert and Denise Gassion. Louis Gassion,

Piaf's father, is said to have fathered as many as nineteen children that he had known about, all of them on the wrong side of the blanket, and what is unfathomable is that only three of these alleged offspring ever came forward, and that none of them—not even Mômone—receive one word of mention in her two volumes of memoirs. All three were disliked intensely by Théo, primarily because they usually only dropped in to see their 'beloved sister' when they wanted something. And while Mômone's book had been a smash hit around the world, Denise Gassion's whitewashed tome detailing Piaf's 'no drugs, no alcohol' life was barely noticed outside of France. As Roger explained:

> It took a lot to make Théo angry, but once you crossed the line that boy had one hell of a temper. He'd been involved in a few brawls before meeting Édith, and certainly knew how to use his fists to look after himself. He loathed Mômone and once said that he'd love nothing more than to strangle 'that fucking bitch' with his bare hands. Théo always believed, as did many of us, that the so-called relatives were all fakes who were not interested in Édith's welfare but only after getting their hands on her money—but that she was terrified of sending them packing in case they spun some yarn about her and Théo and Duggie to the newspapers.

'Duggie' was of course Douglas Davies, who arrived in Paris in April 1962 to stage an exhibition of his works—three of these portraits of Piaf—at a small gallery on the Left Bank. Though no longer amorously interested in him, she insisted upon Doug staying at boulevard Lannes. She hardly ever bore grudges, and was on speaking terms with all of her ex-lovers, even Moustaki. On 20 April, Doug drove her to the studio where she recorded the two songs by Mikis Théodorakis for the soundtrack of the film, *Les amants de Téruel*, which recount the story of the star-crossed lovers whose only way out is suicide, a song which was as morbid as it was beautiful with its amazing trumpet middle section:

> *Retrouvés dans la mort,*
> *Puisque la vie n'a pas su les comprendre ...*
> *Ils dorment délivrés de l'appréhension de l'aube,*
> *Se tenant par la main dans l'immobilité de la prière.*

> [Together in death,
> Since life has failed to understand them,
> They sleep delivered of the apprehension of dawn,
> Holding hands in the stillness of prayer.]

Doug also painted Théo's portrait. But there was more, as Roger explained:

Duggie was the same age as Théo. Some say that Félix Marten was Piaf's tallest man, but this one was even taller. Next to him, she looked like a midget. There was absolutely no rivalry between the two young men. Far from it, for within days Douglas and Théo were sleeping in the same room—and I'm sure that Édith knew, just as she knew about Théo's 'arrangement' with Figus.

On 3 June 1962, Piaf and Théo drove Doug to Orly. He had been scheduled to take an earlier flight, but had swapped his ticket for a seat on Air France Flight 007— among the 130 passengers was a large contingency from the Atlanta Art Association which included a number of his friends, and which had arrived in Paris the previous day on their way back from an extended trip to Rome. Because Piaf hated goodbyes, Doug was dropped off at the entrance, and she was not witness to the terrible tragedy which ensued. The plane crashed on take-off, exploding in a ball of flames at the end of the runway. The only survivors were three stewardesses, one of whom later died at the scene of what was then the worst plane crash in aviation history. The message of sympathy from President Kennedy did not appease Piaf's grief. For the second time, a plane had robbed her of a loved one:

Théo and everyone at boulevard Lannes tried to keep the news from her, until they could find the right moment. Claude Figus told her, though I don't think it was out of spite, and it almost finished her off. Théo didn't see it this way. He kicked him out, and told him that he never wanted to see him again or even hear his name spoken again. Then Édith made Théo swear on the Bible that he would never take a plane …

17: Simone Margantin

Simone Margantin was Piaf's private nurse and carer who entered her employ during the autumn of 1962. The two very quickly became close friends. Édith is said to have appreciated the fact that Margantin never held back when expressing her opinion—and the fact that unlike everyone else at boulevard Lannes, she did not bow and scrape when the 'boss' wanted her own way. Margantin did not approve of Théo Sarapo's way of life—though she did agree that being with him had given Piaf a new, if only temporary, lease of life:

> Théo put it about rather a lot. Boys and girls, they were all the same to him, though he worshipped the very ground that she walked upon. He adored her. It was not fan worship, not hero worship as some said at the time. He wasn't after her money because he knew there wasn't any. Édith had lived extravagantly her whole life, and there had always been hangers-on to help relieve her of her money. Friends who were not really friends at all. Relatives who would have wanted nothing to do with her, had she not been the Great Piaf, and who took

advantage of her being an easy touch. The love that Édith and Théo shared was the blending of two sad souls, which when conjoined could become happy once more. There was never anything physical between the two of them, for no other reason that there could *be* nothing physical because Édith was so very ill. Théo often walked around the place in just his underwear—or if he was walking from the bathroom to the bedroom, wearing nothing at all.

When I spoke to Margantin around 1974 she recalled Piaf saying 'If you've got a good body, show it off —but meaning to boast about it or flaunt it.

Thinking that it would do her good to get away from Paris in the wake of Doug Davies' death, Théo took Piaf to Cannes where they rented a suite at the Hôtel Majestic —not a good idea, considering she had stayed there with Doug, and Théo might have thought otherwise had he known this. It was here on 26 July that he proposed to her. Piaf was stunned. Twenty years and a whole world of experience separated them, and initially she told him that she would need a month to think about it. She then offered him one excuse after another why they should not wed. He was young and handsome enough, she said, to have any woman he wanted, though she was well aware that sexually he was mainly interested in men. And of herself she proclaimed, 'I'm just an old wreck who's cheated on men all my life, an unscrupulous bitch renowned for my capriciousness and foul temper—and one who can't even cook or look after a house.'

Piaf was being ridiculous, for those who knew her were aware that in her whole life she had never washed a cup or picked up a duster. She herself told a reporter that when one of Théo's shirts needed washing, she simply threw it away and bought a new one—additionally, that even in pre-Piaf days when she had been struggling, she had done the same with her daughter Marcelle's nappies. The age-gap *did* worry her, but only because she was afraid of a large part of her more 'fussy' public deserting her should she end up making a fool of herself. There is little doubt, however, that the love she nurtured for Théo more than bordered on the maternal, as she explained to her newest confidant, Jean Noli:

> When I analyze this love, I don't find a mistress's love but something which until now has been refused me—a mother's love. Théo, with his laughter and youthful spirit, gives me the impression at times that I've been given a son. A mother sleeps within even the most voluptuous of mistresses. Only narrow-minded people are offended by what I've done. *I* know that my love of Théo is nothing to be ashamed of.

For decades cynics have asked the same question—why? Piaf was still the highest-paid female entertainer in the world, but spending her fortune as quickly as she earned it. Illness had 'shrunk' her to 4'7"; she weighed just eighty-four pounds, and was so crippled with rheumatism that she found walking an effort. Eating was a horrendous ordeal, and sometimes she had to be fed like a baby. Her doctors reconfirmed that at best she would make it to fifty, and that she might have to stop singing at any moment. So why did Théo, a confessed homosexual, insist on marrying her? Why not allow their affair to run its course like all the others, hopefully grab a successful career out of her, and then move on, that much richer for the experience? Quite simply, he loved her. They adored each other.

The wedding-date was set for 9 October, with Piaf telling friends that this would be sixteen years to the day since she had recorded 'La vie en rose', while cynics observed that on that day too she had recorded 'Mariage' —in which the hapless bride goes to jail for murdering her husband. And once the engagement had been made public, inspired by her new-found joy and helped by her chiropractor, Lucien Vaimber, Piaf began working again. Louis Barrier had arranged a series of recitals on the Côte d'Azur, to be followed by what would be her final season at the Olympia.

They were accompanied by Simone Margantin, who recalled:

> I remember once, they were performing in the South of France. Théo always occupied the first half, then went back on at the end of the evening to sing 'A quoi ça sert l'amour?' During his recital it was incredibly hot, and without thinking what he was doing, Théo whipped off his shirt halfway through a song, and the audience went absolutely wild. After that, Édith encouraged him to remove his shirt during every performance, and it wasn't just the girls who were screaming and swooning. But Édith would never allow Théo to see her naked, and always locked the bathroom door in case he wandered in. No man had seen her naked since Marcel Cerdan, not even Jacques Pills. She was terribly ashamed of her body, with all the scars from the accidents and operations.

Théo's performances were by no means faultless, but they were sincere, unpretentious, and appreciated even by the hordes of media scandalmongers and like any true *chanteur-réalist* he quickly attracted a gay following. Piaf's own recitals were short—sometimes as few as ten songs—and she was so ill that instead of silencing the audience with the customary wave after each song, she allowed it to run on to enable her to recover her strength. Her new songs included

'Fallait-il', 'Une valse', and 'On cherche un Auguste', all performed in the upper register, but the one which stopped the show was Michel Émer's 'A quoi ça sert l'amour?', which proclaimed the couple's private ecstasy to a cynical world. Its alternated couplets form a series of pertinent questions and philosophical response. Théo would ask:

> *A quoi ça sert l'amour?*
> *On raconte toujours les histoires insensées.*
> *A quoi ça sert d'aimer?*

> [What's the point of love?
> One always tells senseless stories.
> What's the point of loving?]

Piaf's response would see her cocking her head on one side whilst gazing up into her Théo's eyes. 'You're the last! You're the first!' And, she concluded:

> *Avant toi y'avait rien, avec toi je suis bien!*
> *C'est toi qu'il me fallait! Toi que j'aimerai toujours!*
> *Ça sert à ça, l'amour!*

> [Before you I had nothing, with you I'm fine!
> You're the one I needed! The one I'll always love!
> That's the point of love!]

The song was introduced on *Cinq colonnes à la une*, a popular television magazine of the day. Piaf, however, was of the opinion that performing a new song in a studio was less satisfactory than airing it before a live audience. She therefore decided that 'A quoi ça sert l'amour?' would have a 'proper' premiere under the most arduous circumstances imaginable, and that Théo, who she felt had got off lightly, performing mostly to tourists in the South, would appreciate 'learning his trade' the hard way—at Chez Patachou, the chanteuse's posh nightclub in Montmartre, an establishment renowned for giving some singers a caustic reception.

Piaf had greatly admired Patachou (1918-2015), one of the finest singers of her generation, until 1954 when Patachou had purloined several of her songs, including 'La goualante du pauvre Jean' and 'Avec ce soleil'. 'I've decided to let her off the hook for all the terrible things she's said about me,' Piaf told Roger Normand, when in fact *she* had done all the insulting over the years. Exactly what Patachou had to say about the matter is not known—she was not in Paris at the time, and Piaf had more than enough to cope with when Théo walked onto the stage and the audience began booing him, and he rushed off in tears. Wearing an old cardigan over her dress and thick woollen socks, Piaf led him back on, and held his hand whilst they sang their song.

The applause was deafening, and she walked off again and he finished his set, with cheers after every song.

The insults, however, were far from over, and the incident at Chez Patachou was followed by a thoroughly heartless and debasing article published in *Noir et Blanc* on 3 August 1962 and which caused Piaf such distress that Théo at once demanded to meet its author, Jean Louville, and give him a good hiding.

EDÍTH PIAF: 'MY MARRIAGE WITH THÉO IS MY CHALLENGE WITH DEATH!

A scrap of cardboard headed HOTEL MAJESTIC, CANNES. Clumsily-written words: Édith PIAF AND THÉO SARAPO HAVE JOY IN ANNOUNCING THEIR MARRIAGE AT THE END OF OCTOBER '62. Signed by the fiancés, this distinctly exceptional, unexpected invitation! The public found it unbelievable when Édith began her 'adventure' with Théo Sarapo, but this marriage exceeds the bounds of understanding. One tries to discern why the *grande chanteuse*, not content with this conspicuous liaison, has to leap the ultimate hurdle and MARRY him. She could easily be his mother, and it is this enormous age difference which shocks us. He is handsome, ambitious. Like others who have become stars, he COULD take her advice and live with Édith for a while, adding a little more to the gossip columns. One can only repeat ... UNBELIEVABLE!

The first thing that offended Théo was the Louville's comment about the 'clumsy' handwriting—the fact was that Piaf was so crippled with rheumatism that writing the note had been a tremendously painful ordeal for her. For years, her friends had been urging her to take legal action against the more scurrilous journalists. She never did, always claiming that even the most disreputable hack had a living to earn, though she did lash out on the radio against a reporter who, seeing her for the first time, dismissed one of her recitals as 'mediocre'— rather unfairly, since she had collapsed on stage at the end of it:

> A journalist goes to see an artiste once, then he goes around saying that he's an experienced critic. This is something for which I reproach him. How dare he reproach me after a single recital. He must come and see me—oh, three or four times before making up his mind. And before he starts pulling me to pieces for not being on form, does he ever stop to think if he's always on cue? Somehow, I don't think so …

While Théo only advocated violence towards detractors, Piaf adopted a less temperamental approach and asked Jean Noli to place an advertisement in *France Dimanche* asking for her public's approval and blessing. In three days, she received over 10,000 letters, cards and gifts from well-wishers. From her suite in the Hôtel Majestic she granted an interview—in English—to Victor Newson of the *Daily Express*, stating that in her 'experienced and unbiased opinion', the British were still not ready to hear her sing because of their 'attitude towards love'. It is thought that she feared being mocked if she sang there now, on account of her relationship with Théo, though they later spent a clandestine weekend in London. Newson delighted her by telling her that he approved of the marriage and wrote, 'The love between Piaf and Sarapo is a love-affair which the whole of France loves.' Even so, she did not change her mind about the British.

Piaf's last season at the Olympia should have been open-ended like the others, but on account of her fragile health Louis Barrier and Bruno Coquatrix restricted it to just two weeks. The Olympia audiences were extremely discerning—even today, major stars have less difficulty filling a 10,000-seater stadium than the 2,000-seater Olympia, and she was still worried what her reception would be when the curtain rose on 27 September. Two evenings prior to this, she gave her last gala performance—a concert from the top of the Eiffel Tower for the premiere of the film, *The Longest Day*. Loudspeakers had been attached to the actual structure, to enable her voice to soar across the rooftops of the city, literally, and as she finished 'Non, je ne regrette rien' the sky exploded in a tremendous display of fireworks. The show was preceded by a sumptuous banquet in the Palais de Chaillot Gardens, and the 3,000-strong audience was the most distinguished she had ever faced: Montgomery and Churchill, the Shah of Iran, Audrey Hepburn and Sophia Loren, the royal families of Greece and Monaco, Maria Callas, Elizabeth Taylor and Richard Burton—and, most important of all, Piaf's friend, President Eisenhower. Of the fourteen songs in her programme, 'Le rendez-vous', 'Toi, tu l'entends pas' and 'Le diable de la Bastille' had been written for her to perform at the Olympia. She also premiered her most portentous song, 'Le droit d'aimer' by Robert Nyel and 'new-kid-on-the-block' Francis Lai, who through her would become a household name. It would become Piaf's personal credo, and it was her last European hit during her lifetime:

> *A la face des hommes au mépris de leurs lois …*
> *Quoi qu'on dise ou qu'on fasse,*
> *Tant que mon coeur battra,*
> *Jamais rien ni personne m'empêchera d'aimer!*
> *J'en ai le droit d'aimer!*

> [Facing men, scorning their laws …
> No matter what anyone says or does,
> So long as my heart's beating,
> Nothing, no one will stop me from loving!
> I have the *right* to love!]

If anyone had the right to love—through fear of losing everything and even at the risk of destroying herself, as Piaf indicated in the song, it was she. As for the Olympia premiere, there was nothing to worry about. Théo was so absolutely petrified when he walked on to the stage that he could be seen to be visibly shaking—his reward was a five-minutes standing ovation *before* starting his set. But the audience was expecting the spectacle of Sarapo, *torse nu,* they were to be disappointed. Piaf had given her fiancé strict instructions to keep his shirt on. Vocally, she was in impeccable form and excelled herself with an even wider range than usual. Francis Lai's 'Musique à tout va', had it been written then, might have defied her during the mid-Fifties when she had been at the peak of her physical powers. Now, it and her other numbers were delivered with relative ease. Her opening song, 'Roulez tambours', was one of the rare protest songs she sang after her visits to America;

> *Pour ceux qui meurent chaque jour,*
> *Pour ceux qui pleurent dans les faubourgs,*
> *Pour Hiroshima, Pearl Harbour!*
> *Pour l'heure et pour la fin des guerres,*
> *Allez, roulez tambours!*

> [For those dying each day,
> For those crying in the suburbs,
> For Hiroshima, for Pearl Harbour!

For the present and for the end of wars,
Come on, roll the drums!]

When Piaf bawled out for Théo to join her on the stage for
'A quoi ça sert l'amour?, there was an outburst of laughter—
perhaps on account of the seventeen-inch difference in
their heights. When they finished the cheers and the wild
applause spoke for itself, and Piaf was more than convinced
that her marriage had been given the invaluable Parisian
seal of approval.

After the premiere, Piaf was interviewed by Pierre
Desgraupes, who had the gall to quiz her about her past
lovers in front of Théo. 'You've had a lot of love in your life,'
he pronounced. 'But one of your lovers stood out from all
the others, didn't he?' Degraupes was referring to Marcel
Cerdan, but Piaf was giving nothing away when she replied,
'There was one. He was genuine. But I'm not going to tell
you who he was.'

Simone Margantin, now her closest female friend,
recalled Piaf's wedding day, a feast for the public and press
alike as 10,000 well-wishers gathered around the Mairie
of the 16th arrondissement: the police had to be drafted in
to restore order before Piaf arrived, wearing a back alpaca
dress—and her old mink coat. She resembled a fragile doll,
but was smiling radiantly on what she declared had been the

happiest day of her life. She had said this when marrying Jacques Pills, but this time she really meant it:

> Édith developed cold feet before the ceremony, and got into such a panic that I had to give her an injection to calm her down. There were tremendous problems with Claude Figus … While Édith and Théo had been engaged, he had continued to be Théo's lover, and suspecting that all this was going to change once Piaf had the ring on her finger, he'd gone to the press with stories about him and Théo and some of the things they had got up, before and since meeting Piaf. But, in the end, all turned out well. Édith and Théo weren't together for very long after their wedding—one year and a day—but it was a happy marriage, I'm certain of that.

For Claude Figus, there would be no happy ending. On 5 September 1963 he was found dead in his Saint-Tropez hotel room. The official verdict was that he had taken a drugs overdose, some said in a fit of remorse after being ousted by Piaf. An article in *Paris Match*, seven years later as part of Théo Sarapo's obituary, suggested that Figus may even have been murdered. This would have surprised few of those who knew him, considering the crowd he mixed with outside the Piaf household.

18: Claude Sounac

Claude Sounac was a member of the Claude Figus-Théo Sarapo clique, who later went on to co-found Les Amis d'Édith Piaf, and who was present when Édith was 'knocking Théo into shape' on the eve of Olympia '62:

> Most of the people privileged to sit in on the rehearsals believed he would never make it. Théo used to stand there, looking as though he had shit himself and singing down his nose all the time. He really was quite dreadful. But Louis Barrier [Piaf's manager] quite rightly thought that, as lacking in talent as he was, he would pull in the crowds because of the scandal of his being attached to Piaf. Many venues took him on just to humour her. And Édith was so *aggressive* with him that Théo would burst into tears and beg her to stop. I'm surprised he didn't change his mind about marrying her, she was so harsh with him. I'm sure he must have been thinking, 'My God, what's it going to be like after October?' On one occasion she kept him on his feet for eight hours without a break. And yet, amazingly, by the time she'd finished with him, he *really* could sing.

And brief as it was, theirs was a gloriously happy marriage because after years of drifting from one man to another, Piaf had found her guardian angel.

19: Elisabeth Welch

■　　■　　■

Elisabeth Welch (1904-2003) was an American singer whose career spanned over seventy years. She very kindly wrote the preface to my book, *Piaf: A Passionate Life*, in 1998. She was only the second black artiste, after Joséphine Baker, to appear in Paris at the Moulin Rouge. Her most celebrated songs were Cole Porter's 'Love For Sale', 'Stormy Weather', which she memorably performed in Derek Jarman's 1979 film, *Tempest* ... and, 'La vie en rose'.

> I like to think that I helped introduce the British to Édith Piaf's work. I was doing a revue in London, and the producer wanted a show-stopper, so I suggested 'La vie en rose'. He was quite horrified when I said that I wanted to sing it properly, in the original French, instead of using the Kennedy translation, 'Take Me To Your Heart Again'. London audiences weren't all that sophisticated in those days, and he said the public wouldn't know what I was singing about. I argued that hardly anyone understood what was being sung in opera, but that it didn't stop them from enjoying it. So I did the song, and it was a big hit.

I never met Piaf, more's the pity. I flew on the same plane as her when she came to London for a private show at the Mayfair Hotel, I saw her many times in Paris, and I saw her again in America when they'd made her feel very uncomfortable by turning her into a Hollywood-style 'glamour-puss', though I can understand her mentality for allowing them to do that when you think of what she came from. I even appeared on the same bill as her, at the Olympia when she was with the Greek boy, Théo Sarapo, towards the end of her life. She was very sick, then, and disorientated. He had to follow her on to the stage and turn her around to face the audience. By this time I was used to the shock— and it was a shock—of seeing the spot move over to the wings and picking up this little thing in a black serge dress and flat, tied-up shoes, the sort schoolgirls used to wear. She looked like something off the streets, no make-up, only bright red lipstick, her hair an absolute mess. I never saw such a sight. But when she opened her mouth—my God, the beautiful sound that came out, and the way you saw only her hands and her face when she was singing. It was the most astonishing thing I ever witnessed in my life. And believe me, I've seen them all.'

20: Simone Berteaut (Mômone)

■ ■ ■

Soon after her wedding, Piaf entered a detoxification clinic: through no fault of her own, she had again become dependent on the needle. Fortunately, the visit was brief and when she returned to her apartment, accompanied by Simone Margantin who would stay by her side until the end, she seemed strong enough to take on her next venture—a short season in Brussels at L'Ancienne Belgique, an establishment like the Olympia known for its frequently tetchy audiences. For days, whilst rehearsals were taking place, boulevard Lannes was busier than it had been on the eve of Olympia '61, with a seemingly incessant stream of media interviews. This time Piaf had less patience. It had taken her thirteen years to replace Cerdan—if indeed she had—and for the first time she branded some reporters 'vultures' to their faces. She took others for a ride. One young man amused her, and needless to say his name was never revealed:

TO THEO: What effect will it have on you,
marrying a woman twenty years your senior?

RESPONSE: Édith has the character of a child …

TO PIAF: What effect does it have on you,
marrying a man twenty years younger than
yourself?

RESPONSE: The effect that I was lucky to find a
man who's so gentle … and handsome.

TO THEO: Will you have any children?

RESPONSE: If my wife wishes …

TO PIAF: Do you want to have children?

RESPONSE: Sure. Why not!

Piaf's tour proved too much for her, but she stuck it out
even though she was twice rushed back to Paris to be given
vital blood transfusions. In Brussels she premiered 'Le chant
d'amour', which she had written with Charles Dumont. She
later claimed that whilst writing it she had seen beyond her
own death—for the lovers in the song, herself and Théo,
both die and are reunited in heaven to share the same griefs.
On 12 December she gave a splendid recital at Nijmegen,
in Holland. This was filmed for a television broadcast, aired
on the 14th, and to date remains the only complete filmed
Piaf recital known to exist.

For Piaf, time was swiftly running out, yet she was still convinced that her precognitive dream would see her through the very worst of her traumas. She and Théo opened at the Bobino on 18 February 1963 in a series of recitals which could almost be compared with the wave of Beatlemania which swept across the word later that year—even Théo received a twelve-minute standing ovation before being allowed to sing. Eight of his twelve songs were written by Piaf, including the somewhat over-strident 'Défense de', an attack on the *honourable société* which according to the song are intent on banning everything, including love. As an introduction to another proposed tour of Britain which would not take place—Piaf said she had commissioned an English lyric which is yet to come to light—there was 'Un dimanche à Londres'. The inspiration for this had come from a clandestine visit to London, shortly before her marriage, when the city had been enshrouded in fog. The public and most of the critics observed that Théo's act was more polished than it had been at the Olympia.

Piaf's opening performance was more hysterically received than any other she ever gave—at one stage the fans became so rowdy that the theatre staff braced themselves for a riot and thought about calling the police. The public, as if aware that they were hearing the Great Piaf for the last time, went mad. One song drove them into a frenzy, and was even more disturbing than 'Les blouses blanches'.

'C'était pas moi', by Robert Gall and Francis Lai, was acted out so dramatically that the audience was convinced she was having a fit. Even now it is impossible to hear it without feeling that 'something' has walked over one's grave. It tells the story of a man who has been thrown into a prison for a murder he did not commit, and has to be heard to be believed. And finally she sang 'Les gens', a subtle slap in the face for those who still criticized her marriage:

> *Comme ils baissaient les yeux les gens,*
> *Comme ils nous regardaient les gens,*
> *Quand tous deux on s'est enlacé,*
> *Quand on s'est embrassé ...*

> [How the people lowered their eyes,
> How the people looked at us when we hugged,
> When we kissed each other ...]

After the Bobino, Piaf and Théo toured again, though by now she was so ill that it was an effort to sing more than ten songs, and as with her previous tour she had to keep returning to Paris for medical treatment. The public were ready to believe that she would go on forever, for she had already announced that she would never retire. And of course she was only forty-seven, the age when most *chanteuse-réalistes* are reaching their peak.

Then on 18 March 1963, Édith Piaf sang in public for the last time, at the Opera House in Lille—and it was at around this time, according to Simone Berteaut, that her doctors discovered that she was suffering from cancer of the liver, too far advanced to effect a cure.

I met Simone Berteaut (1916-75) shortly before her death, and she was a very strange woman indeed. By this time she was heavily reliant on alcohol and medication, her speech was slurred and her movements erratic—even so, I came away from our meeting convinced that she really could have been Piaf's half-sister, and not the impostor others had accused her of being.

Simone Berteaut's relationship with Piaf appears to have been a veritable rollercoaster of ups and downs. Mômone, as Piaf nicknamed her, was present at every important event in her life, either helping or—more often than not—hindering. In 1969, she caused a tremendous controversy when she published *Piaf*, a kiss-and-tell which recounts Piaf's story, warts-and-all. French fans were shocked, but as the ensuing years have proved, much of what Mômone wrote had actually happened—there was precious little embellishment and invention on the author's part. In Britain, Pam Gems turned the story into a massively successful play, *Piaf*, with Jane Lapotaire in the title-role and, some years later, Elaine Paige. Absolutely *no* musical theatre production about Piaf—staged anywhere in the world, not just in France—has had the same degree of success as Pam Gems' masterpiece.

On a less controversial note, in 1974 parts of it were tamed down and used as the basis for a film. *Piaf* (UK: *Piaf The Early Years*) was ably directed by Guy Cazaril, and starred twenty-year-old Brigitte Ariel—Betty Mars performed Piaf's earlier songs, and did so inordinately well. Her rendition of 'Comme un moineau' is definitive. The story covered Piaf's life until her 1940 triumph at the ABC, where she performed 'L'accordeoniste'.

Mômone did not mince words when talking about her detractors, and what they had put her through:

> I didn't steal from anyone. I didn't kill anyone. I wrote a book to the best of my ability. I had nothing to gain by making up stories. Édith and I shared the same father but, thank fuck, we didn't share the same mother, though my own mother was not much better than hers, just an old drunken bitch who would sleep with anyone so long as they were plying her with drinks. People dragged me through the shit for getting there first and writing what they were afraid to write. If they had a problem with my story, that was their problem, not mine. Édith was involved with some wonderful people, but she was also involved with more than a few creeps. Only

one man besides Cerdan was worthy of her—Théo
Sarapo. The others were mostly shits who used her
for what they could get out of her. They didn't like
what I wrote about them because they didn't like
reading the truth.

Mômone was being hypocritical, for she had taken
advantage of Piaf's overt generosity more than anyone. On
a number of occasions she had stolen from her, attempted
to sell stories about her to the press, and caused a great
deal of friction between Piaf and her friends and lovers.
Yet curiously, she had always been forgiven. Some twenty
years after Mômone's death, I met her daughter—a chip off
the old block who at the time owned a fashion shop near
Les Halles, in the centre of Paris. She had no problem with
me publishing our interview at some future date, she said,
though she did ask me not to refer to her by name:

> When my mother's book was published, everyone
> was so spiteful towards her. Many fans were still
> angry that the Church had denied Piaf a Christian
> burial because, according to them, she had lived a
> life of public sin. My mother's book had revealed
> everything—and it was all true. Was she Piaf's
> sister? She said so, and I believed her … She said that
> Louis Gassion had accepted her as his daughter. No
> one ever seemed to doubt the paternity of Herbert
> Gassion, but my mother always believed that Denise

Gassion was a fake. What she told you was correct. Some of those celebrities called Simone Berteaut a liar and a charlatan because they didn't want the world to know what *they* had really been like. And how many of them have since been revealed to have had what you would call 'regular' private lives— staying with the same wife or not cheating on her, or not being involved in some scandal or other? I can't think of a single one.

Mômone's book pulls no punches, and despite the adverse criticism sold well over a million copies in France alone. And once one reaches page 50, one does not care *what* Piaf got up to away from the concert platform and the recording studio: the story is so riveting. Mômone presents Piaf as the archetypal heroine, a latter-day Joan of Arc, while bringing some of the men in her life down to the slug's-belly level they deserved. Louis Leplée *had* been a procurer of rent-boys. Raymond Asso *had* been a near-psychotic Svengali—Piaf *had* been so headstrong, she had needed to be badgered into place, though Asso had been wrong to abuse her physically. Yves Montand *had* cheated on her with another man. Piaf *had* tried to take Cerdan away from his wife, Jacques Pills *had* been an opportunist creep. Moustaki and Félix Marten *had* beaten her senseless. Théo Sarapo *had* been her salvation, and not interested in marrying Piaf for her money, well aware that her only legacy would be a mountain of debts.

Piaf's last few months saw her drifting from coma to coma, hardly recovering from one relapse before having another. A tape-recorder was always kept next to her bed and there was always someone close at hand to play the piano, if she had the strength to sing. On good days, she talked excitedly about a proposed tour of Germany—her first visit since singing for the prisoners during the war. She had already made a demonstration tape of 'Non, je ne regrette rien', sung phonetically in German. She had never forgiven the Germans for their atrocities during the Occupation, and Charles Dumont and Michel Vaucaire had written 'Le mur', a harrowing song about the Berlin Wall. Piaf taped this in vocalese, along with their 'Mikael'—the former would be handed over to Barbra Streisand, three years after Piaf's death, and recorded in French and English versions. On 7 April, Piaf taped 'L'homme de Berlin', by Francis Lai and Michelle Vendôme, with Lai accompanying her on the accordion and Noel Commaret—her orchestra leader from the Bobino recitals—on the piano. It is perhaps ironic that her very first and last commercial recordings should take on the well-rehearsed Piaf subject of prostitution. The woman has just arrived in Berlin, searching to find a way of forgetting. She sees a man through the drizzle, and standing under the grimy, anxiously weeping sky, she imagines that life with him would work out fine if only she were not in Berlin. One wonders what the Germans would have thought of the song and Piaf's interpretation, had she sung it there:

> *Ne me parle pas de Berlin,*
> *Puisque Berlin n'a rien pour moi!*
> *Y'a pas qu'un homme dans ce foutu pays,*
> *Il n'y a pas que lui …*

> [Don't speak to me about Berlin,
> For Berlin has nothing for me!
> There's only one man in this fucking country,
> There's only him …]

Mômone's daughter recalled the only time she ever met Piaf, in 1963 shortly before her death:

> Piaf knew that she did not have much time left. That's why, during the summer of 1963, she sent for Raymond Asso, and begged him to help her, as he had helped her before. My mother said that when Asso had turned up, she had asked him to take her away from the circus, as she called it, and that Asso had agreed.

On 10 April 1963, three days after recording 'L'homme de Berlin' Piaf developed an oedema of the lung and lapsed into a coma. Upon her recovery, Théo Sarapo took her to Cap Ferrat, where he rented a villa close to the sea. Piaf had indeed sent for sixty-two-year-old Asso, himself ailing. Théo's wanting to be away from Paris was two-fold, for he had started being pestered by journalists about his life before meeting Piaf. One seems to have been told—by Claude Figus, who had been paid handsomely—of Théo's involvement with Douglas Davies. Once again, Théo threatened to employ his fists but was stopped by Piaf, who paid the man to keep quiet. Was Piaf worried about what would happen, should the press print a story that Théo had once worked as a male prostitute? Was she actually thinking of *leaving* him? Asso seems to have believed so. Writing in the notes of booklet for *De la Môme à Édith*, the boxed set of four albums which offered a retrospective of her formative years, he observed:

> I will not dwell on the lamentable picture that I saw. Sumptuously clean, surrounded by a pitiful band of clowns like in a Pirandello drama, I discovered an absolutely unrecognizable Piaf. She took me to one side, and weighed her words carefully. 'Raymond, it's very bad. I think I'm done for, this time. Perhaps I still have a chance, with you. Now that you're free, when I return to Paris you must come and live with me and rid me of all this trouble—of all these

people around me.' '*All* of them?' I asked. 'Yes,' she
said. 'All except for Loulou.'

'Loulou' was her manager, Louis Barrier. But was Piaf
being serious? Asso almost certainly knew nothing about
Théo's past, but the press was awash with stories of his
protectiveness—the fact that some believed he might have
been killing her with kindness, having been told by her
doctors that she might not have long to live. According to
Asso, she *had* been planning to leave Théo, at the end of
October, and set up house with her former mentor—even if
she *was* on the verge of death, he said, at least with him she
would be able to die in an atmosphere of serenity.

There seems of course little doubt, given Piaf's track-
record, that if she had not been so desperately ill, the
marriage to Théo would not have lasted. She was too set
in her ways to ever change. Between relapses she rehearsed
new songs—almost exclusively by Charles Dumont, though
Jacques Brel had composed 'Je m'en remets à toi' especially
for her. There would be no more studio recordings—just
the handful of previously mentioned taped rehearsals.

Eventually, because the sea air was proving too much for
her, Théo took Piaf to Gatouniere, a mountain retreat near
Mougins. In the middle of August she lapsed into a hepatic
coma—this time the doctors told Théo to prepare himself
for the worst. Miraculously, she still clung to life and upon

her discharge Théo took her to Plascassier, a village near Grasse. The house he rented here, l'Enclos de la Bourre, was described by one of her friends as 'the most depressing prison on God's earth'. Confined to a wheelchair at times, Piaf was frequently too ill to be aware of her surroundings. Théo too was absent much of the time. The director Georges Franju had offered him one of the leads in *Judex*, which necessitated on his making regular trips to Paris. Piaf would not hear of him sacrificing his career just to look after her when she had a capable nurse [Simone Margantin], and as an actor he showed great promise.

But if Mômone had always admired Théo and considered him the only worthwhile and unselfish man Piaf had ever had since Marcel Cerdan, the feeling was not mutual. Mômone maintained that she had informed Piaf of Claude Figus's death—not out of spite, but because Piaf had kept asking where he was, and therefore needed to be told the truth. In 1948, when Piaf had been with Cerdan, the 'demon spirit' had stolen some of Cerdan's letters to Piaf and tried to sell them first to Cerdan's wife, and then to the press. There had been an almighty bust-up, and Mômone had taken Cerdan to court, accusing him of hitting her. Within the court-house, she had dropped the case, and while Cerdan had stomped off in a huff, Piaf and Mômone had emerged, linking arms and smiling radiantly for the press as if nothing had happened.

At the end of September 1963, when Mômone arrived at L'Enclos de la Bourre with her daughter, 'on the cadge', as Piaf put it, Théo had not revised his opinion about wanting to strangle her with his bare hands. According to Piaf's nurse, Simone Margantin, *she* had turned Mômone away, only to be overruled by Théo, who had allowed her inside the sickroom for just two minutes, as a last resort to get rid of her. Mômone told a different story, as did her daughter:

> My mother said that the nurse was a bitch, but that she supposed she was only doing her job. There was hardly any light in the room—it was really gloomy. Édith was in the bed, and Théo was stretched across the foot of the bed like a long, faithful dog. My mother and Édith began reflecting about the past, about all their adventures and the scrapes they had been in. When their talk started to get dirty, I left them to it and went for a walk into the village. I returned an hour or so later. Théo was still in the same position, and I guess his eyes must have been really opened by some of the stories he'd heard. My mother later said that Édith's last words to her had been, 'Watch out for yourself, Mômone. In this life you only pay for the stupid things you do.' She wrote in her book that she had also said, 'I can die now—I've lived twice!'—but I can't recall her telling me that at the time.

21: Jacqueline Danno

■ ■ ■

Never overtly fond of other female singers, Piaf had taken
Théo Sarapo's younger sister, Christie Laume, under
her wing—some believed more as a favour to Théo than
an act of recognition of Laume's insipid voice at a time
when pretty singers of dubious talent and longevity were
emerging on both sides of the Channel at an alarming rate,
and floundering just as quickly. Laume opened the show at
some of Piaf's and Théo's recitals, but she never made any
great impression and it would take until 1966, this time
with Théo's intervention, for her to acquire a recording
contract. Over the next three years she released a number of
EP's, but none of these were successful.

One young singer who Piaf very much admired during
the spring of 1963—one who possessed sufficient genuine
talent to get her to the top, as opposed to 'family-related
warblings'—was Jacqueline Danno. A former student with
Mireille's Petit Conservatoire de la Chanson, she is also
my very dear godmother, and today one of France's most
acclaimed and respected actresses. Piaf had been impressed
by her 'Chez Lolita', written by Claude Delécluse, whose

'C'est à Hambourg' and 'Les amants d'un jour' had been worldwide hits for Piaf. She had also been 'bowled over' by Jacqueline's 'Mere Douloureuse'—from the pen of Gilbert Bécaud, this tells of a mother's grief after finding her twenty-year-old son's body at the bottom of a ravine. 'Formidable,' Piaf told the composer. 'Danno's found a new way to die! Get her to come and see me!' The meeting took place, but could have ended in disaster, as Jacqueline explained:

> I had been the first to record Dumont's 'Les amants', and I was terrified in case this was brought up. It was, and she stunned me by telling me that my version was better than hers—such a *compliment*. Then we discovered that we had something else in common other than our record producer, Jacques Poisson—'Mister Fish', she called him. This was our birth-signs. Piaf was obsessed with birth-signs and omens, and said that was the luckiest in the zodiac, followed by Capricorn—Marlene's and Jesus's sign. After that I visited the apartment every week, until later that summer when Théo took her to the South. The last words she said to me were, 'Don't forget our dinner-date when I get back from my holidays.' Throughout her whole life she had believed in miracles, and I'm sure she was convinced that she'd beaten her illness.

Between bouts of unconsciousness, Piaf made the best of her time at Plascassier, begging Théo to take her back to Paris as soon she was strong enough to travel. During the afternoon of 20 September she was still feeling very optimistic when she gave what would be her last press interview, to *France-Soir*:

> Evidently there are always going to be these minor setbacks, though at the moment I'm very well and expect to be back in Paris in about a month's time. There are going to be lots of new songs—I'm preparing for a new series of recitals. I've seen my doctor, and he changed my medication. It cost me a lot of money, but right now I'm fine. I expect to be recording in a couple of months, all being well …

On 9 October 1963, their first wedding anniversary, Piaf sent Théo a card upon which she had scrawled, 'I don't deserve a man like you—yet you're here all the same.' It was while he was reading this, at the villa in Plascassier, that she lapsed into the hepatic coma from which she never emerged. Simone Margantin was at her bedside when, at around midnight, her condition became critical and she suffered an internal haemorrhage. There was a storm brewing and the doctor, who in any case would not have been able to save her, could not reach the villa until five the next morning. When he arrived he confirmed the worst: the world's greatest ever *chanteuse-réaliste* was dying. At noon, Margantin asked Danielle Bonel, Piaf's secretary and the wife of Marc, her accordionist, to call a priest. Tragically, because of the storm she was unable to get through on the telephone. The faithful, loving nurse spoke of Édith's last moments with infinite tenderness: At ten minutes past one her eyes opened—they seemed to be shining. Then they closed again, and her head drooped forwards.

Piaf herself had once said, 'I'm determined to come back to earth after my death.' She was just forty-seven years old, but during her last year had looked much older. Though she actually died on 10 October, the newsflashes did not go out until seven the next morning. Édith Piaf, who had loved Paris like a lover, could not die in some provincial village, severed from her second heart—the people would never have forgiven her. Aware that they were breaking the law, Théo and Margantin travelled overnight with her body in the back of an ambulance. In her hands was a spray of mimosa which was preserved and kept by Théo for several years. Back at boulevard Lannes, Piaf was laid in state in her vast salon, her coffin surrounded by her *fétiches*: the statuette of Saint Theresa, an epaulette from a légionnaire's coat, letters from Marlene, Cerdan and Cocteau, a sailor's beret given to her in 1936 when she had visited Brest, and a rabbit's foot. These items would all be buried with her.

Though advised not to do so for fear of there being a riot, Théo opened the doors of the apartment to the crowd: *la foule,* that contingent of unseen lovers to whom Piaf had cried, 'I love you! You are my life!' For two days, a constant stream of people filed past her coffin, draped with the French flag as a tribute to all she had done for her country in helping Jewish prisoners-of-war to escape from the Nazis. There was a further irony the next day when Jean Cocteau succumbed to a heart-attack while preparing a eulogy for Piaf to be read over the radio.

Piaf was buried in the Père Lachaise cemetery on Monday 14 October, amidst one of the most emotional scenes Paris has ever seen. Her funeral remains the largest there has ever been for a popular personality. Two *million* people lined the streets of the city along the funerary route, and as the cortège filed past—eleven cars piled fifteen feet high with flowers, the people fell to their knees. Within the cemetery, 40,000 people clambered over the gravestones, causing no little damage. Beside the grave, a detachment from the Foreign Legion stood to attention and gave a salute of honour. Their enormous wreath of purple wild flowers was inscribed, 'A leur Môme Piaf—La Légion'.

The Catholic Church afforded Piaf the supreme insult by denying her the Requiem Mass, declaring she had lived a life of public sin—atrocious, in that this would not have happened today. A priest, Père Thouvenin, and Bishop Martin kindly said prayers over Piaf's grave, to an unearthly silence. Théo could barely stand, and had to be supported by Louis Barrier. Marlene arrived alone—she was wearing no make-up and carrying a single rose. Simone Berteaut, still craving attention, pushed her way to the front row of mourners which comprised Marlene, Charles Aznavour, Herbert and Denise Gassion, Jacques Pills, Charles Dumont, Marcel Cerdan Jr, Gilbert Bécaud, Les Compagnons, Théo's parents and sisters, and almost every one of the Piaf Boys— not in her favourite blue this time, but in black.

For a week, Théo shut himself away in his room—the household staff were not allowed near him, the telephone left off the hook. Then, on 22 October—flinging open the shutters and opening the curtains—he set about fulfilling dinner engagements Édith had arranged before leaving Paris. Jacqueline was one of the first visitors:

> It was both strange, and moving. No kinder, more generous a person than Théo has ever walked this earth, and the poor boy was *lost*. Everything in the apartment was exactly as Édith had left it, save for the living room, where every wall was covered in her photographs and posters. And at the head of the dining table, her place had been set as usual— only on her chair he had placed the mimosas which

she had clasped in her dead hands during that last journey back to Paris. I felt so *numb*, watching him, that I could hardly eat. Even now I'm unable to remember who else was sitting at that table … It was soon after that dinner that all the staff were forced to leave. Poor Théo couldn't afford to keep them on, and they were just as distressed to be leaving him as he was, having to let them go.

22: Madame Leclerc

■　　　■　　　■

Madame Leclerc was the self-appointed 'caretaker' of Piaf's grave during the Seventies—a sweet but feisty old dear who though a massive Piaf admirer often took exception to her being the centre of attention where visitors to Père Lachaise were concerned. Hail, rain or shine, she could be found hovering around the 97th Division regaling the tourists with stories about Théo, for whom she had had a soft spot.

> I never regarded Édith as Théo's wife, but as a surrogate mother. There could never be a physical relationship between them, and I don't think either of them ever expected there to be. She was too ill, too frail for that kind of thing. But they loved each other very much, of this there was absolutely no doubt. Théo was so besotted with her that, had she asked him to throw himself off the top of the Eiffel Tower, he would have done so without hesitation. I only met Édith once, and very briefly—outside the church on the day of her marriage. I met Théo properly for the first time early one morning when he came to place flowers on her grave. He was heartbroken, and I invited him here [to her apartment at 72 rue de Bagnolet]. After that he

visited me regularly, and once he found out that he could trust me, he started bringing his friend.

Madame Leclerc never named Théo's lover, believed to have been either Claude Sounac or one of his friends, and I never pressed.

They appeared to be in love, but I got the impression that it was more a physical relationship than the deep bond that Théo had formed with Édith.

On Christmas Eve, purposely ill-timed, the bailiffs turned up at boulevard Lannes and drew up a list of items to be sold to pay off some of Piaf's debts. Amongst the items seized was an abstract painting by the Russian-born artist, André Lanskoy. This was bought back and returned to Théo by André Schoeller, the director of a gallery in the rue de Miromesnil. Schoeller was now revealed to have secretly offered Piaf a 'shoulder to cry on' during her affair with Moustaki. Schoeller originally bought the painting as a gift for her: she had insisted on paying him for it, and there had even been talk of him moving in with her, and her adopting his child. For the last few years of her life the painting had hung over the television set in her room.

Théo was still saddled with an immense legacy of debts, which under Gallic law he was obliged to pay— and pay them he did. Between 1963 and 1970 he toured constantly and was not always well-received, with the shouts of 'gigolo' ringing in his ears until he had paid most of them off. *Judex*, his film with Georges Franjus, was not the commercial success everyone had expected. In 1964, he honoured a contract with the Bobino which had been signed the previous year, and aware that he was not yet ready for top-billing he pleaded with the manager of the theatre to be 'demoted' to *vedette-américane* to someone else. Appallingly, there was not one artiste in France who would agree to appear with him, and he battled through his short season of recitals alone. One song endeared him to his limited public. Written by Noel Commaret and Francis Lai, 'La maison qui ne chante plus' may now be regarded as Théo Sarapo's epitaph:

> *Je partirais de la maison … qui ne chante plus.*
> *Je n'aurais plus l'horizon*
> *Pour toujours que le monde inconnu.*
> *Je fermerais la porte sur elle, et notre amour …*

> [I will leave the house … which sings no more.
> My horizon evermore will be
> The unknown world.
> I will close the door on her, and our love …]

Théo recorded some very fine songs, and his voice improved considerably with each new record release: Édith's influence, even from beyond the grave, afforded him only the best writers and composers. His last hit in France was ironically entitled 'Oui, je veux vivre'—*Yes, I want to live*. On 28 August 1970, shortly after recording the song, he was killed in a car crash outside Limoges, and it has subsequently proved difficult to prove that this was not suicide—close friends have stated persistently that Piaf's death had robbed him of the will to go on living. He sleeps next to her in the 97th Division at Pere Lachaise, in the same tomb which holds the remains of Édith's beloved father and baby daughter.

Afterword

■ ■ ■

In the half-century since her death, there have been numerous contenders for the Piaf crown. Artistes like Patachou, Juliette Gréco, Cora Vaucaire, Pia Colombo, Colette Renard and Catherine Sauvage were unique whilst Piaf was alive, and for many years continued the *chanson-réaliste* tradition which is becoming increasingly moribund now that the intimacy of the music hall has given way to the greed-inspired world of the stadium and the television talent contest. A few years after Piaf's death, a trio of 'sound-alikes' emerged: Betty Mars, Georgette Lemaire and Mireille Mathieu. Betty was the more convincing because, like Piaf, she was a true *enfant du faubourg*. In recent years, there is scarcely a major female singer in Europe who has not attempted Piaf, often with woeful results, and almost always to cash in on some anniversary or other. Perhaps the only ones worthy of note are Michelle Torr, and the great Italian diva, Milva, whose album of Piaf songs comes pretty close in quality, power, and depth of feeling to the real thing. I defy anyone to listen to her thrilling rendition of 'Hymne à l'amour' without a shudder. In France, the only true *chanteuse-réaliste* after Piaf was Barbara, whom some believe actually surpassed her, but only in France—like her alter-idol she always refused to sing in Britain, even though she asked me to adapt several of her songs into English. A tireless campaigner against injustice, the death penalty, sexual and racial prejudice, and for AIDS awareness, Barbara died in November 1997, leaving a nation—and myself—in perpetual mourning.

There have been biographies galore, frequently covering the same ground and saying little more than we know already, most especially in France where Piaf's story has almost invariably—Simone Berteaut apart—been presented as a 'hearts and flowers' romance, as opposed to how it really was. When Piaf sang 'Non, je ne regrette rien', she was proclaiming to the world that she regretted nothing whatsoever, neither the good nor the bad, and neither should we wish to see her in blinkered vision.

It is also impossible to keep track of the record releases. Almost every CD released contains the regular fare of 'Milord', 'La vie en rose', etc, yet every one sells thousands of copies just the same. Occasionally, a record company will come up with a gem—such as the release, for the fiftieth anniversary of Piaf's death, of an album containing songs impounded by the German authorities during the German Occupation of Paris—or Piaf's appearances on *La joie de vivre*, the French equivalent of Britain's *This Is Your Life*.

Surprisingly, there is much unreleased material in the archives, such as Piaf's US television appearances with the likes of Patti Page. One hopes that these will resurface some day.

Piaf's life—mostly highly fictionalized—has been covered in three films. A year or so before her death, Simone Berteaut sold the rights to her book. The ensuing production, *Piaf* (UK: *Piaf The Early Years*) was not a resounding success, but it was a fine film all the same, covering Piaf's discovery by Louis Leplée, and ending with her 1940 Bobino triumph, where she introduced 'L'accordéoniste'. Playing Piaf was an unknown actress, Brigitte Ariel. Many of her songs in the film were performed by Betty Mars because the original recordings were too worn to be transferred. Her version of 'Comme un moineau' is so breathtakingly superb, it brings tears to the eyes. Sadly, in February 1989, finding the pressures of life too hard to bear, Betty took her own life. Claude Lelouche's *Édith et Marcel*, telling the story of Piaf and Cerdan and featuring Evelyne Bouix and the boxer's son, Marcel Cerdan Jr, was poor by comparison. Bouix looked nothing like Piaf, and her onstage movements were not just contrived, they were embarrassing to watch. The greatest film tribute without *any* doubt is *La Mome* (UK: *La Vie En Rose*), directed by Olivier Dahan and featuring Marion Cotillard as Piaf. The scriptwriters did not quite get it right—there was too much emphasis on Piaf's childhood, no mention of the war or of Théo Sarapo, allegedly because a member of his family had not wanted him in it, but Cotillard's portrayal of Piaf was so perfect that it was inevitable it would win her an Oscar, which it did.

There have also been many fine television tributes, though for many in Britain the first will always remain the best. *I Regret Nothing*, produced for the BBC by Michael Houldey, included tributes from lovers, composers and friends, and featured Jacques Pills' final television appearance, just weeks before he died. Théo Sarapo was approached to appear, but refused.

In Britain, the Piaf legacy has been best-preserved on the stage in the most unusual manner courtesy of Pam Gems, who was the first to admit that writing *Piaf*, which initially starred Jane Lapotaire, as 'utter madness'. In her play, Gems equates Piaf's Belleville *argot* with Cockney, and throws in a good many four-letter words for good measure. In the original version, her first words upon stomping on to the stage—when she sways back and forth in front of the microphone and someone rushes to her aid—are 'Get yer fucking hands off me.' Elsewhere she shouts and screams, and even urinates, yet in a strange way the play never comes across as vulgar. In recent years, the most famous 'Piaf' has been Elaine Paige. Her 'Mon Dieu' alone was worth the exorbitant tickets prices at London's Piccadilly Theatre.

Perhaps the last word should be left to Charles Aznavour, who observed, 'For most of us, Piaf is not dead. For those of us who loved her, and there are many, she will live on in our hearts until the end. Piaf was not an ordinary mortal—she was a *monster-sacré* who lived, sang and loved like no other mortal before her. She was unique.'

Édith Piaf Discography

■ ■ ■

1935-45 Polydor;
1946-63 Pathé Marconi;
1947-8 Decca;
1956 CBS (USA).

A complete guide to the recorded output of Édith Piaf which includes lyricists, composers, tape recordings (TR), acetates (AC) and live recordings (LR) of songs not recorded in the studio. The dates refer to the actual recording sessions and are not release dates. In her formative years, Piaf often worked with musicians and orchestras provided by the studio. Between 1946 and 1962, however, her musical director was Robert Chauvigny, and unless otherwise stated it is he who was responsible for her arrangements and accompaniment during these years.

1935

15 October — *La java en mineur* [1] (Léo Poll, Raymond Asso, Marcel Delmas. TR made in Marie Dubas' dressing room, ABC Theatre. Piano: Raymond Asso.

18 December — *Les mômes de la cloche* [1, 2 & 3] (Decaye, Vincent Scotto).

La java de Cézigue (Eblinger, Groffe).

Mon apéro (Robert Juél, Robert Malleron, Marguerite Monnot).

L'étranger [1, 2 & 3] (Robert Malleron, Robert Juél, Marguerite Monnot. Piano: Marguerite Monnot.

1936

10 January — *Les hiboux* [1] (Joullot, Dalbret) Accompanied by Les Accordéons Médinger.

15 January — *La fille et le chien* [1] (Jacques-Charles, Charles Borel-Clerc, Charles Pothier. Piano: Raymond Asso.

Je suis mordue (Jean Lenoir, L Carol, R Delamare) Accompanied by Les Accordéons Médinger.

Reste [1] (Will Léardy, Pierre Bayle, Jacques Simonot). Piano: Raymond Asso.

7 March — *Mon amant de la Coloniale* (Raymond Asso, Robert Juél).*

24 March — *Fais-moi valser* [1 & 2] (Charles Borel-Clerc, Telly.*

Va danser (Maurice Legay, Gaston Couté).*

La Julie Jolie (Léo Daniderff, Gaston Coute).*

Quand-même (Louis Poterat, Jean Wiener, J Mario) Piano: Jean Wiener.

The latter from the film, *La Garçonne.*

31 March — *La fille et le chien* [2] Piano: Jacques-Charles. Guitar: Django Reinhardt.

7 May — *Les deux ménétriers* [1 & 2] (Jean Richepin, Louis Durand.*

Il n'est pas distingué (Paul May, Marc Hélly)**

8 May — *Y avait du soleil* (Jean Lenoir)**

23 October — *'Chand d'habits* [1 & 2] (Jacques Bourgeat, R Alfred).**

28 October — *La petite boutique* (Roméo Carlés, O Hodeige).**

*Orchestra : Emile Stern.

** Orchestra: Georges Aubanel.

1937

28 January — *Le contrabandier* (Gilles, Raymond Asso).**

Ne m'écris pas [1 & 2] (René Cloerec, Louis Lagard, Jean Rodor).*

Mon légionnaire [1 & 2] (Raymond Asso, Marguerite Monnot)*

Le fanion de la Légion [1 & 2] (Raymond Asso, Marguerite Monnot)*

The verse has a different melody to the 'regular' version.

12 April — *Corrèque Et Réguyer* (Paul May, Marc Hélly).***

Dans un bouge du vieux port (André Liaunet, André Deltour)***

Entre Saint-Ouen et Clignancourt (Adelmar Sablon, André Mauprey)*** with

Maurice Alexander on accordion.

Mon coeur est au coin d'une rue (Henri Coste, Albert Lasry).***

24 June   *C'est toi le plus fort* [1] (Raymond Asso, René Cloerec)****

Browning (Gilles, Raymond Asso)****

Paris-Méditerranée (Raymond Asso, René Cloerec)****

Un jeune homme chantait [1 & 2] (Raymond Asso, Léo Poll)****

12 November   *Ding din don* [1 & 2] (Raymond Asso, Pierre Dreyfus)****

Tout fout le camp [1& 2] (Raymond Asso, Robert Juél)****

Le fanion de la Légion [3] 'regular' version.****

16 November   *Le chacal* [1 & 2] (Raymond Asso, Charles Seider, Robert Juel)****

J'entends la sirène (Raymond Asso, Marguerite Monnot)****

Le mauvais matelot [1] (Raymond Asso, Pierre Dreyfus)****

Partance [1 & 2] (Raymond Asso, Léo Poll)****

The last two songs are duets with Raymond Asso.

*Orchestra: Emile Stern.

**Orchestra: Georges Aubanel.

*** Orchestra: Wal-berg.

On the Wal-berg recordings Piaf is billed 'Édith Piaff'.

**** Orchestra: Jacques Métehen

1938

15 March   *Le fanon de la Légion* [3]*

Madeleine qu'avait du coeur [1] (Raymond Asso, Max d'Yresne)**

Les marins ca fait des voyages (Raymond Asso, Mitty Goldin)**

On the last two recordings Piaf is billed 'Édith Piaff'.

September   *Le fanion de la Légion* [4] AC*

Madeleine qu'avait du coeur [2] AC*

3 October   *C'est lui que mon coeur a choisi* (Raymond Asso, Max d'Yresne)**

Le grand voyage du pauvre nègre (Raymond Asso, René Cloerec)**

Madeleine qu'avait du coeur [3]

Le mauvais matelot [2] Solo version**

12 November   *Mon légionnaire* [3 & 4]** Solo violin thought to be Stephane Grapelli.

November   *La java en mineur* [2] Piano: Raymond Asso. Full-length version.

*Orchestra: Wal-berg.

** Orchestra: Jacques Métehen

1939

31 May   *Les deux copains* (Raymond Asso, Charles Borel-Clerc)*

Je n'en connais pas la fin (Raymond Asso, Marguerite Monnot)*

Le petit monsieur triste (Raymond Asso, Marguerite Monnot)*

Elle fréquentait la rue Pigalle (Raymond Asso, Marguerite Monnot)*

*Orchestra: Jacques Métehen

1940

18 March
C'est la moindre des choses [1] (Paul Misraki)*

Sur une colline (Paul Misraki)*

20 March
C'est la moindre des choses [2] AC*

On danse sur ma chanson (Raymond Asso, Léo Poll)*

Y'en a un de trop (Édith Piaf, Marguerite Monnot)*

The latter, written by Piaf as 'Un coin tout bleu', was given by her to Damia. Piaf therefore wrote an alternative lyric for herself.

5 April
L'accordéoniste [1] (Michel Émer)**

Elle fréquentait la rue Pigalle [2] AC**

Embrasse-moi [1 & 2] (Wal-berg, Jacques Prévert)**

Jimmy c'est lui [1] (Kamke, Wal-berg) Duet with Adrian Lamy**

27 May
L'accordéoniste [2]** Accordion: Gus Viseur.

This is the version usually issued on Philips-Polydor compilations.

Embrasse-moi [3] AC*

Escale [1 & 2] Jean Mareze, Marguerite Monnot)*

Jimmy, c'est lui [2] **

C'était la première fois (Édith Piaf, Marguerite Monnot) AC*

*Orchestra: Jacques Métehen

**Orchestra: Wal-berg

1941

27 May
C'était un jour de fête [1 & 2] (Édith Piaf, Marguerite Monnot)*

Ou sont-ils mes petits copains? [1 & 2] (Édith Piaf, Marguerite Monnot)*

C'est un monsieur très distingué (Édith Piaf, Louiguy)*

J'ai dansé avec l'amour [1] (Édith Piaf, Marguerite Monnot)*

November
L'homme des bars (Édith Piaf, Marguerite Monnot)**

The latter two songs from the film *Montmartre-sur-Seine.*

*Orchestra: Jacques Métehen

**Orchestra: Johnny Uvergolts

1942

9 February
Le vagabond [1] (Édith Piaf, Louiguy)*

Sung with Yvon Jean-Claude & Claud Normand Ensemble.

13 November
Les hiboux [2]*

Le vagabond [3]* AC

25 November
Simple comme bonjour (Roméo Carlés, Louiguy)**

Written for *Montmartre-sur-Seine*, but dropped.

Un coin tout bleu (Édith Piaf, Marguerite Monnot)**

See also 20 March 1940.

Tu es partout (Édith Piaf, Marguerite Monnot)**

The latter two songs from *Montmartre-sur-Seine*.

1 December	*Le vagabond* [3 & 4]*** Solo versions.
15 December	*C'était une histoire d'amour* [1 & 2] (Henri Contet, Jean Jal)* Duet with Yvon Jean-Claude, later sung in the film *Etoile sans lumiere*.
31 December	*Le disque usé* [1] (Michel Émer)***

J'ai qu'a l'regarder [1 & 2] (Édith Piaf, Alex Siniavine)***

*Orchestra: Claude Normand

** Orchestra: Johnny Uvergolts

*** Orchestra: Paul Durand

1943

| 2 January | *Je ne veux plus laver la vaiselle* (Henri Contet, Marguerite Monnot)* |
| 8 January | *Le brun et le blond* (Henri Contet, Marguerite Monnot)* |

C'était si bon (Henri Contet, Marguerite Monnot)*

La valse de Paris (Édith Piaf, Marguerite Monnot)*

La demoiselle du cinquième (Henri Contet, Louiguy) AC*

| January | *Y'avait ses mains* (Édith Piaf, Raymond Asso)* |

| 18 January | *Le disque usé* [2] As Version 1. AC. |

Tu es partout [2] As Version 1. AC.

| 10 February | *Monsieur Saint-Pierre* [1 & 2] (Henri Contet, Johnny Hess)** |

Version 2 with children's choir.

| 14 March | *Chanson d'amour* (Henri Contet, Marguerite Monnot)** |

Monsieur Saint-Pierre [3, 4 & 5]**

| 7 April | *C'est l'histoire de Jésus* (Édith Piaf, Marguerite Monnot) AC*** |

Mon amour vient de finir (Édith Piaf, Marguerite Monnot) AC***

Written for *Montmartre-sur-Seine*, but dropped when Piaf gave the song to Damia.

| 24 April | *Histoires de coeur* (Henri Contet, Marguerite Monnot, based on a concept by Édith Piaf)*** |

*Orchestra: Paul Durand

** Orchestra: Guy Luypaerts

***Orchestra: Claude Normand

1944

| 20 January | *Un monsieur me suit dans la rue* (Jean-Paul Lechanois, Jacques Besse)* |

Also features Georges Bartholé on piano.

| 21 January | *Coup de grisou* [1 & 2] (Henri Contet, Louiguy)* |

Two versions exist of Version 1, which runs at 4'20. The one frequently released runs at 3'18 minus the lengthy introduction.

27 January — Le chasseur de l'hotel [1, 2 & 3] (Henri Bourtayre, Henri Contet)*

C'est toujours la même histoire (Daniel White, Henri Contet)*

13 May — Les gars qui marchaient (Henri Contet, Marguerite Monnot)*

14 May — Celui qui ne savait pas pleurer (Henri Contet, Claude Normand)*

Il riait (Georges Bartholé, Henri Contet)*

Regarde-moi toujours comme ca (Henri Contet, Marguerite Monnot)*

26 June — De l'autre coté de la rue (Michel Émer)*

Escale [2]*

4 July — Y a pas de printemps [1] (Henri Contet, Marguerite Monnot)*

The 'regular' version at 2'37. See also 9/3/46.

Les deux rengaines (Henri Bourtayre, Henri Contet)*

*Orchestra: Guy Luypaerts

1946

9 March — Y a pas de printemps [2]

Longer (4'35) version with extra verse and chorus. LR, Radio Suisse- Romande. Accordion: Marc Bonel. Piano: Robert Chauvigny.

23 April — Adieu mon coeur (Henri Contet, Marguerite Monnot)*

C'est merveilleux (Henri Contet, Marguerite Monnot)*

Le chant du pirate (Henri Contet, Marguerite Monnot)*

All from the film Etoile sans lumiere.

May — Johnny Fedora et Alice Bonnet-Bleu (Allie Weubel, Édith Piaf, Ray Gilbert).

'Mixed' to include backing from the Andrews Sisters for the film,

La boite a musique (US: Make Mine Music). Orchestra unknown.

4 June — Miss Otis regrette (Cole Porter, Henneve, Palex)

Monsieur est parti en voyage (Stephen Beresford, Jacques Larue)

Both LR, Radio Suisse-Romande. Piano: Robert Chauvigny.

25 June — Céline (Traditional)

Dans les prisons de Nantes (Traditional)

La complainte du roi Renaud (Traditional)

Le roi a fait battre tambour (Traditional)

All four arranged by Marc Herrand and Louis Liebard. Sung a cappella with Les Compagnons de la Chanson.

Les trois cloches (Gilles)

Sung a cappella with Les Compagnons de la Chanson. From the film, Neuf garçons, un cœur.

9 October — Je m'en fous pas mal (Michel Émer)*

Mariage (Henri Contet, Marguerite Monnot)*

213

From the film, *Etoile sans lumiere*.

Le petite homme (Henri Contet, Marguerite Monnot)*

La grande cité (Édith Piaf, Marguerite Monnot) AC*

Un refrain courait dans la rue (Édith Piaf, Robert Chauvigny)*

La vie en rose [1] (Édith Piaf, Louiguy)*

The last two songs from the film, *Neuf garçons, un cœur*.

6 December	*Une chanson à trois temps* [1] (Anna Marly)*
7 December	*C'est toi le plus fort* [2]**

Sans y penser (Norbert Glanzberg)**

Dans ma rue (Jacques Datin)***

La fille en bleue (Traditional)

The latter performed *a cappella* with Les Compagnons de la Chanson. All four LR, Radio Suisse-Romande.

*Orchestra: Guy Luypaerts

**Piano: Norbert Glanzberg

***Piano: Jacques Datin

1947

6 January	*Le rideau tombe avant la fin* (Jean-Marc Thibault, Jacques Besse)*

Elle avait son sourire (Daniel White, J P Laseyres)*

Both LR, Radio Suisse-Romande.

6 February	*Les cloches sonnent* (Édith Piaf, Marguerite Monnot)**

Le geste (Michel Émer)**

Monsieur Ernest a réussi (Michel Émer)**

Si tu partais [1] (Michel Émer)**

7 February	*Une chanson à trois temps* [2]**

Sophie (Édith Piaf, Norbert Glanzberg)**

From the film, *Neuf garçons et un coeur*.

6 October	*Douce nuit* (F Gruber, Jean Brousolle) AC.

Sung *a cappella* with Les Compagnons de la Chanson.

Qu'as tu fait, John? (Michel Émer)*

7 October	*C'est pour ca* [1] (Henri Contet, Marguerite Monnot)*

Sung with Les Compagnons de la Chanson. From the film,

Neuf garcons et un coeur.

Un homme comme les autres (Édith Piaf, Pierre Roche)*

October	*Un air d'accordéon* (Michel Émer) AC, no other details.

Clair de lune (Traditional) AC, no other details.

Black Boy (Michel Émer) AC, no other details.

*Orchestra: Guy Luypaerts

** Orchestra: Raymond Legrand

1948

11 June	*Monsieur Lenoble* (Michel Émer)*

Boléro (Henri Contet, Paul Durand) AC*

Les amants de Paris (Léo Ferré, Eddie Marnay)*

Il pleut (Charles
Aznavour, Pierre Roche)*

12 July   *Monsieur X* (Michel
Émer, Roger Gaze)**

Les vieux bateaux
(Jacques Bourgeat,
Jacqueline Batell)**

21 July   *Il a chanté* (Cécile
Didier, Marguerite
Monnot)*

Duet with Marcel Jiteau.

6 August   *Amour du mois de mai*
(Jacques Larue, Norbert
Glanzberg)**

Cousu de fil blanc
(Michel Émer)**

*Orchestra: Guy
Luypaerts

** Orchestra: Raymond
Legrand

In 1948, whilst deciding
whether or not to extend
her Decca contract, or
to record exclusively
for Pathé-Marconi, Piaf
made acetates and tape-
recordings of a number
of songs which were
released by neither. The
details are sketchy:

Studio unknown, May:
Sans faire de phrase;
*Y'avait une voix qui
se lamentait*; *Pourquoi
m'as-tu trahi?*; *Les yeux de
ma mere*; *Le routier* (all
written by Édith Piaf,
Marguerite Monnot).
No other details.

Decca, 12 July: *Blues
de février*; *Monsieur
Lévy*; *Pas une minute
de plus*; *Vol de Nuit* (all
written by Édith Piaf,
Marguerite Monnot).
Orchestra unknown,
possibly Raymond
Legrand.

Unknown: *Blues
d'octobre*; *Le pauvre*

homme (both by Michel
Émer). No other details.

Unknown: *J'ai dansé avec
l'amour* (with amended
lyrics); *Moi je sais qu'on
se reverra*; *Le gilet* (all
written by Édith Piaf,
Marguerite Monnot).
Orchestra unknown,
possibly Guy Luypaerts.

Unknown: *Poker*
(Charles Aznavour,
Pierre Roche). No other
details.

1949

Orchestra: Robert
Chauvigny, unless
otherwise stated.

3 February   *Dany* (Édith Piaf,
Marguerite Monnot).

Le prisonnier de la tour
(Francis Blanche, Gérard
Calvi)

Paris (André Bernheim)

From the film, *L'homme
aux mains d'argile*.

9 February   *Tu n'as pas besoin de
mes rêves* (Édith Piaf,
Marguerite Monnot).

Pour moi toute seule
(Michel Philippe-Gérard,
Flavien Monod, Guy
Lafarge).

1 March   *Bal dans ma rue* (Michel
Émer).

21 July   *L'orgue des amoureux*
(Francis Carco, André
Varel, Charlie Bailly).

Pleure pas (Henri Contet,
Aimé Barelli)

December   *You're Too Dangerous,
Cheri* (Édith Piaf). LR,
Copacabana Club, Paris.

The first English version
of *La vie en rose*, written
by Piaf in 1948 for

Gracie Fields. Wrongly dated as July 1949. White introduces Piaf on Stage with *White Christmas*.

1950

| 2 May | *Hymne à l'amour* (Édith Piaf, Marguerite Monnot). |

From the film, *Paris chante toujours*.

| 11 May | *La petite Marie* (Édith Piaf, Marguerite Monnot). |

| 19 June | *Tous les amoureux chantent* (Jean Jeepy, Marguerite Monnot). |

Le ciel est fermé (Henri Contet, Marguerite Monnot).

| 20 June | *La fête continue* (Michel Émer). |

Il fait bon t'aimer (Jacques Plante, Norbert Glanzberg).

Le chevalier de Paris (Angele Vannier, Michel Philippe-Gérard).

Grand Prix du Disque, 1952.

| 7 July | *C'est un gars* (Charles Aznavour, Pierre Roche). |

C'est d'la faute à tes yeux (Édith Piaf, Robert Chauvigny).

| 8 July | *Hymn To Love* [1] (Édith Piaf, Marguerite Monnot, Eddie Constantine). |

English adaptation of *Hymne à l'amour*.

Just Across The Way (Michel Émer, Christopher Hassall) AC.

English adaptation of *De l'autre coté de la rue*.

The Three Bells (Gilles, Bert Reisfeld).

Solo version, English adaptation of *Les trois cloches*.

La vie en rose [2] (Édith Piaf, Louiguy, Mac David).

English adaptation, 'drums' version.

If You Go (Michel Émer, Geoffrey Parsons) AC & LR.

English adaptation of *Si tu partais*.

All My Love (Paul Durand, Mitchell Parish) AC & LR.

English adaptation of *Boléro*.

| 10 July | *Il y avait* (Charles Aznavour, Pierre Roche). |

Simply A Waltz (Norman Wallace) LR, with applause removed.

An original song, never performed in French, written for Piaf to sing

Before General Eisenhower.

| 11 July | *Don't Cry* [1] (Édith Piaf, Eddie Constantine). |

English adaptation of *C'est de la faute a tes yeux*.

'Cause I Love You [1] (Édith Piaf, Eddie Constantine).

English adaptation of *Du matin jusqu'au soir*.

| July | *Je n'attends plus rien* [1] (Meleville, Guillermin, Cazaux). TR. |

Le dénicheur [1] (Gibert, Agel, Daniderff) TR.

Les feuilles mortes (Joseph Kosma, Jacques Prévert) AC.

French (as opposed to later French & English) version.

1951

6 April — *Demain il fera jour* [1] (Marcel Achard, Marguerite Monnot)*

11 April — *Du matin jusqu'au soir* (Édith Piaf)*

L'homme que j'aimerais (Marcel Achard, Marguerite Monnot)*

13 April — *Si si si* (Marcel Achard, Marguerite Monnot)*

Duet with Eddie Constantine

Avant l'heure (Marcel Achard, Marguerite Monnot)*

Rien de rien (Charles Aznavour, Pierre Roche)*

15 April — *Chanson bleue* [1] (Édith Piaf, Marguerite Monnot).

Du matin jusqu'au soir [2] LR.

Broadcast from Orly airport. Piano: Marguerite Monnot.

Dans tes yeux (Édith Piaf, Marguerite Monnot) TR*

Written for *La p'tite Lili* but discarded.

La valse de l'amour (Édith Piaf, Marguerite Monnot)*

C'est toi [1] (Édith Piaf, Marguerite Monnot) Solo version.*

C'est toi [2] Duet with Eddie Constantine. Sung in French & English.*

*From the operetta, *La p'tite Lili*.

4 July — *Chante-moi* (Édith Piaf) Duet with Marcel Jiteau.

Une enfant (Charles Aznavour, Robert Chauvigny).

15 October — *Plus bleux que tes yeux* (Charles Aznavour).

Je hais les dimanches (Charles Aznavour, Florence Véran).

Padam, padam (Henri Contet, Norbert Glanzberg)

8 November — *Jézebel* (Wayne Shanklin, Charles Aznavour).

La chanson de Catherine (Pierre Damine, Joumiaux, Youri).

Grand Prix Concours de Deauville, 1951.

La rue aux chansons (Michel Émer).

23 November — *Noël de la rue* (Henri Contet, Marc Heyral).

A l'enseigne de la fille sans coeur (Gilles).

25 November — *Télégramme* (Michel Émer).

1952

May — *Leyi M'Plorer* (*Gilles a perdu*) TR, sung in Flemish.

28 June — *Mon ami m'a donné* (Raymond Asso, Claude Valéry).

Au bal de la chance (Jacques Plante, Norbert Glanzberg).

Je t'ai dans la peau [1] (Jacques Pills, Gilbert Bécaud).*

3 September — *Les amants de Venise* [1 & 2] (Jacques Plante, Marguerite Monnot).

Version 2 has an extra couplet at the end.

Bravo pour le clown (Henri Contet, Louiguy).

Jean et Martine (Michel Émer).

Pour qu'elle soit jolie ma chanson (Édith Piaf, Louiguy).*

Duet with Jacques Pills.

11 December *Et moi* (Michel Émer),

Soeur Anne (Michel Émer).

N'y va pas Manuel (Michel Émer).

Le diable est près de moi (Édith Piaf, Marguerite Monnot) AC.

*From the film, *Boum sur Paris!*

14 December *L'effet qu'tu me fais* (Édith Piaf, Marc Heyral)

Cri d'amour (André Varel, Charlie Bailly) AC.

24 December *Heureuse* [1] René Rouzaud, Marguerite Monnot),

Johnny tu n'es pas un ange (Les Paul, Francis Lemarque).

1954

16 February *La goualante du pauvre Jean* (René Rouzaud, Marguerite Monnot).

10 April *Le 'ça ira'* [1] (Ladré, Bécourt). Sung with male voice choir.

Le 'ça ira' [2] Solo version.

From the film, *Si Versailles m'était conté.*

20 October *Avec ce soleil* [1 & 2] (Jacques Larue, Michel Philippe-Gérard).

Sous le ciel de Paris [1] (Jean Dréjac, Hubert Giraud). Sung with choir.

Sous le ciel de Paris [2] Solo version.

27 October *Mea culpa* (Michel Rivgauche, Hubert Giraud).

Enfin le printemps (René Rouzaud, Marguerite Monnot).

23 November *L'homme au piano* (Henning & Terningson, Jean-Claude Darnal).

13 December *Sérénade du pavé* (Jean Varney). Created by Eugénie Buffet in 1895.

From the film, *French Can-Can.*

19 December Medley: *Le dénicheur/Je n'attends plus rien/J'en ai passé des nuits*. TR.

Sung in a Paris street. Accordion: Maurice Alexander.

Tous mes rêves passés (Édith Piaf, Marguerite Monnot).

1955

27 January *L'accordéoniste* [3] LR, Paris Olympia.

This version, with the applause edited out, is the best-known.

Légende [1] (Édith Piaf, Gilbert Bécaud) LR, Paris Olympia.

28 February *C'est à Hambourg* (Michele Senlis, Claude Delécluse, Marguerite Monnot).

Le chemin des forains (Jean Dréjac, Henri Sauget).

Un grand amour qui s'achève (Édith Piaf, Marguerite Monnot).

Miséricorde (Jacques Larue, Michel Philippe-Gérard).

La vida en rosa Spanish & French version of *La vie en rose*. LR.

Mexican television, Spanish lyricist unknown.

1956

4 January	*Allentown Jail* (Irving Gordon) TR, Carnegie Hall rehearsal.
8 February	*Les amants d'un jour* (Michele Senlis, Claude Délecluse, Marguerite Monnot).
	Soudan une vallée (Charles Meyer, Biff Jones, Jean Dréjac).
28 February	*L'homme à la moto* (Jerry Lieber, Mike Stoller, Jean Dréjac).
8 March	*Avant nous* (René Rouzaud, Marguerite Monnot).
20 June	*Toi qui sais* (Michel Émer).
	Une dame) Michel Émer).
4 July	*Et pourtant* (Michel Émer, Pierre Brasseur).
	Marie la Française [1 & 2] (Jacques Larue, Michel Philippe-Gérard). Version 2 has a different musical arrangement.
	Dis-moi (Charles Aznavour, G Wagenheim) AC.
11 July	*Heaven Have Mercy* (*Miséricorde*).*
	One Little Man (*Le petite homme*)*
	I Shouldn't Care (*Je m'en fous pas mal*)*
	*English lyrics by Rick French.
	My Lost Melody (*Je n'en connais pas la fin*) English lyrics: Harold Rome.
	La vie en rose [3] English version, without drums.

Hymn To Love [2].

'Cause I love You [2].

Don't Cry [2]

Autumn Leaves English lyrics: Johnny Mercer.

Suddenly There's A Valley (Charles Meyer, Biff Jones) LR, US television.

Chante-moi, Darling Sing To Me (*Chante-moi*) English lyrics: Mac David.

16 November	*Une jeune apatride* (Édith Piaf, Marguerite Monnot) LR.*
	Pleine de nostalgie (Édith Piaf, Marguerite Monnot) LR.*
	Le lapin et les chameaux (Robert Juél, Raymond Asso) LR.*

*Recorded at the Porte St Jean, Quebec, Canada.

1957

13 January	*C'est pour ça* [2] LR*
	Je t'ai dans la peau [2] LR*
	Les grognards [1] (Pierre Delanoe, Hubert Giraud). LR*
	Heureuse [2] LR*
	Lovers For A Day (*Les amants d'un jour*) English lyrics: Rick French. LR
	The Highway (*Un jeune homme chantait*) English Lyrics: Rick French. LR
	La vie en rose [4] LR*.
	If You Love Me, Really Love Me (*Hymne à l'amour*) English lyrics: Geoffrey Parsons. LR.

All the above performed at Carnegie Hall.* Sung in French & English.

September	*I'll Remember Today* (Édith Piaf, William Engvick) LR.
	Written by Piaf for Patti Page. Performed live on US television.
25 November	*La foule* (Angel Cabral, Michel Rivgauche.
	Les grognards [2] (Pierre Delanoe, Hubert Giraud).
	Studio version, sung in French.
	Opinion publique (Henri Contet, Marguerite Monnot),
	Salle d'attente (Michel Rivgauche, Marguerite Monnot).
	Les prisons du roi (Irving Gordon, Michel Rivgauche).
	French adaptation of *Allentown Jail.*
7 December	*Comme moi* (Michele Senlis, Claude Delécluse, Marguerite Monnot).

1958

21 March	*Mon manége à moi* [1 & 2] (Jean Constantin, Norbert Glanzberg).
27 March	*Les amants de demain* (Henri Contet, Marguerite Monnot)*
	Fais comme si (Michel Rivgauche, Marguerite Monnot)*
3 July	*Un étranger* [1] (Georges Moustaki, Norbert Glanzberg).
	Le ballet des coeurs (Michel Rivgauche, Norbert Glanzberg).
2 September	*Les neiges de Finlande* (Henri Contet, Marguerite Monnot)*

	Tant qu'il y aura des jours (Henri Contet, Marguerite Monnot)*
3 September	*C'est un homme terrible* (Jean-Pierre Moulin).
	Le gitan et la fille (Georges Moustaki).
	Les orgues de barbarie (Georges Moustaki).
	Eden Blues (Georges Moustaki).
	Un etranger [2] (Georges Moustaki, Evan, Robert Chauvigny).
	Different melody than the one issued regularly on compilations.
4 September	*Je me souviens d'une chanson* (Jean-Pierre Moulin, Félix Marten).
	Tatave (Albert Simonon, Henri Crolla).
	Je sais comment (Julien Bouquet, Robert Chauvigny).
	Mon amour je t'aime (Michel Rivgauche, Marguerite Monnot) TR.
	When The World Was Young (*Le chevalier de Paris*) TR.
	Recorded in New York. English lyrics: Johnny Mercer.
	*From the film, *Les amants de demain.*

1959

January	*Faut pas qu'il se figure* [1] (Michel Rivgauche, Georges Moustaki) TR.
24 February	*Milord* (Georges Moustaki, Marguerite Monnot, Rick French) LR.*
	The Gypsy (George Moustaki, Rick French)*

Jean l'Espagnol (*Madame la Vierge-Marie*) TR, New York.

5 August · *Milord* (Georges Moustaki, Marguerite Monnot) Sung in French.

T'es beau tu sais (Henri Contet, Georges Moustaki).

*Sung in English on *The Ed Sullivan Show*, New York.

1960

January · *C'est l'amour* [1] (Édith Piaf, Marguerite Monnot) TR.

Piano: Marguerite Monnot

April · *Embrasse-moi* [4] Piano: Robert Chauvigny. TR.

13 May · *Ouragan* (Claude Léveillé, Michel Rivgauche).

C'est l'amour [2] Studio version.

20 May · *Les amants merveilleux* (Robert Gall, Florence Véran).

Cri du coeur (Jacques Prévert, Henri Crolla).

Je suis à toi (Julien Bouquet).

Le vieux piano (Henri Contet, Claude Léveillé).

27 May · *Le long des quais* (Henri Contet, Claude Leveillé) TR.

Rue de Siam (Henri Contet, Claude Léveillé) TR.

Boulevard du Crime (Michel Rivgauche, Claude Léveillé).

October · *Les mots d'amour* [1] (Michel Rivgauche, Charles Dumont) TR.

Archived as *C'est fous que j'peux t'aimer.*

10 November · *Non, je ne regrette rien* (Michel Vaucaire, Charles Dumont).

La vie, l'amour [1 & 2] (Michel Rivgauche, Robert Chauvigny).

24 November · *Les mots d'amour* [2].

Jérusalem (Jo Moutet, Robert Chabrier).

December · *Kiosque à journaux* [1 & 2] (Pierre Lacotte, Michel Rivgauche, Claude Léveillé)*

Le métro de Paris [1 & 2] (Pierre Lacotte, Michel Rivgauche, Claude Léveillé)*

Non, la vie n'est pas triste (Édith Piaf, Claude Léveillé)*

*These songs, extracts from the ballet, *La voix*, were recorded on tape and released posthumously.

12 December · *Mon Dieu* (Michel Vaucaire, Charles Dumont).

Des histoires (Michel Vaucaire, Charles Dumont).

15 December · *La ville inconnue* (Michel Vaucaire, Charles Dumont).

Je m'imagine (Nita Raya, Marguerite Monnot).

22 December · *T'es l'homme qu'il me faut* [1 & 2] (Édith Piaf, Charles Dumont).

La belle histoire d'amour (Édith Piaf, Charles Dumont).

Les flons-flons du bal (Michel Vaucaire, Charles Dumont).

29 December   *Les blouses blanches*
(Michel Rivgauche,
Marguerite Monnot) LR.
Sung at the Paris
Olympia.

1961

25 January   *Toujours aimer* (Nita
Raya, Charles Dumont).

Dans leur baiser [1 &
2] (Michel Vaucaire,
Charles Dumont).

Mon vieux Lucien
(Michel Rivgauche,
Charles Dumont).

3 February   *Marie-Trottoir* [1 &
2} (Michel Vaucaire,
Charles Dumont).

Exodus [1 & 2] (Eddy
Marnay, Ernest Gold).

Version 2 has a different
arrangement.

2 March   *Le billard électrique*
(Louis Poterat, Charles
Dumont).

Faut pas qu'il se figure
[2] (Michel Rivgauche,
Charles Dumont).

The version released by
Pathé-Marconi, though
Piaf always sang the
Moustaki version on
stage.

13 March   *Mon Dieu* (Charles
Dumont, Dallas) English
version.

In Jerusalem (*Jérusalem*)
English lyrics: Dallas.
TR.

No Regrets (*Non, je ne
regrette rien*) English
lyrics: Hal David.

23 March   *Le bruit des villes*
(Louis Poterat, Charles
Dumont).

C'est peut-être ça [1]
(Michel Vaucaire,
Charles Dumont). TR.

Piano: Charles Dumont.

4 April   *Carmen's Story* (Michel
Vaucaire, Charles
Dumont) Sung in
French.

*Qu'il etait triste cet
anglais* (1 & 2) (Louis
Poterat, Charles
Dumont).

Sung partly in English.

C'est peut-être ça [2]
Studio version.

C'est peut-être ça [3]
Studio version with
choir.

17 April   *Les amants* (Édith Piaf,
Charles Dumont) Duet
with Charles Dumont.

May   *Non, je ne regrette rien*
(lyricist unknown) Sung
in German. TR.

Les bluets d'azur (Jacques
Larue, Guy Magenta)
TR.

Quand tu dors [1 &
3] (Jacques Prévert, C
Verger) TR.

1962

26 January   *Fallait-il* [1 & 2] (Michel
Vaucaire, Charles
Dumont).

Toi tu l'entends pas [1
& 2] (Pierre Delanoe,
Charles Dumont).

15 February   *Une valse* [1 & 2]
(Jacques Plante, Charles
Dumont).

Polichinelle [1 & 2]
(Jacques Plante, Charles
Dumont).

On cherche un auguste
(Robert Gall, Charles
Dumont).

19 April   *Inconnu excepté de Dieu*
(Louis Amade, Charles
Dumont).

Duet with Charles
Dumont

20 April	*Les amants de Těruel* (Jacques Plante, Mikis Théodorakis)*	
	Quattorze juillet (Jacques Plante, Mikis Théodorakis)*	
4 May	*Le petit brouillard* (Jacques Plante, Francis Lai).	
3 September	*Musique à tout va* (René Rouzaud, Francis Lai).	
	Emporte-moi (Jacques Plante, Francis Lai).	
	À quoi ça sert l'amour? [1] (Michel Émer) Duet with Théo Sarapo.	
	À quoi ça sert l'amour? [2] Solo version.	
20 September	*Légende* [2] Satirical version. Piano: Noël Commaret. TR.	
	*From the film, *Les amants de Těruel*.	
	Le diable de la Bastille (Pierre Delanoe, Charles Dumont).	
	Le droit d'aimer [1] (Robert Nyel, Francis Lai).	
	Orchestra: Jean Léccia.	
21 September	*Roulez tambours* (Édith Piaf, Francis Lai).	
13 November	*Le droit d'aimer* [2] Orchestra: Robert Chauvigny.	
3 December	*Le rendez-vous* [1] (René Rouzaud, Francis Lai).	
12 December	*Le rendez-vous* [2] New arrangement. LR, Nimegue, Holland.	
December	*Les amants du dimanche* (Édith Piaf, Francis Lai) TR.	

1963

January	*Les filles d'Israel* (Georges Moustaki) TR.

18 February	*Les gens* (Michèle Vendôme, Francis Lai)*
	C'était pas moi (Robert Gall, Francis Lai)*
	Monsieur Incognito (Florence Véran, Robert Gall)*
	Traqué (Florence Véran, Robert Gall)*
	J'en ai tant vu (Michel Émer)*
	Tiens v'la un marin (Julien Bouquet)*
	Le chant d'amour (Édith Piaf, Charles Dumont)*
	Margot Coeur-Gros (Michèle Vendôme, Florence Véran)*
	LR Bobino Music-Hall. Orchestra: Noel Commaret.
7 April	*L'homme de Berlin* (Michèle Vendôme, Francis Lai) TR.
	Accordion: Francis Lai. Piano: Noël Commaret. Piaf's last official recording, first released 1968.
June	*Un dimanche à Londres* (Édith Piaf, Florence Véran). TR.
	Duet with Théo Sarapo. Piano: Noël Commaret.
August	*Un jour* (Georges Moustaki) TR*
	Je m'en remets de toi (Jacques Brel) TR*
	Le mur (Michel Vaucaire, Charles Dumont) TR*
	Michael (Michel Vaucaire, Charles Dumont) TR*
	*Recorded in Cannes.

223

The Vinyl Recordings:

Worldwide, Piaf's (and Théo Sarapo's) most sought-after—and frequently most expensive recordings have been the extended-play and ten-inch LPs released in France between 1952 and 1972. All are long-since deleted, and are as follows:

Édith PIAF EXTENDED PLAY

SCRF 103:	Je t'ai dans la peau; Monsieur et Madame.
SCRF 121:	Bravo pour le clown; Les amants de Venise
SCRF 126:	Les croix; Jean et Martine.
SCRF 134:	La goualante du pauvre Jean; Soeur Anne.
SCRF 141:	Mea culpa; Enfin le printemps.
SCRF 446:	Mon Dieu; Des histoires.
ESRF 1022:	La goualante du pauvre Jean; Heureuse; Johnny tu n'es pas un ange; Soeur Anne.
ESRF 1023:	Padam padam; Jezébel; Mariage; Les amants de Venise.
ESRF 1036:	C'est à Hambourg; Le chemin des forains; L'homme au piano; Retour.
ESRF 1051:	La vie en rose; Les trois cloches; Hymne à l'amour; L'accordéoniste.
ESRF 1070:	Soudain une vallée; L'homme à la moto; Avant nous; Les amants d'un jour.
ESRF 1135:	Les grognards; Les prisons du roi.
ESRF 1136:	La foule; Comme moi; Salle d'attente.
ESRF 1174:	Mon manège à moi; Fais comme si; Le ballet des coeurs; L'étranger.
ESRF 1197:	*Édith Piaf Chante Jo Moustaki*: Eden Blues; Les orgues de barbarie; Le gitan et la fille. Sleeve notes: Georges Brassens.
ESRF 1198:	*Édith Piaf Chante Les Airs du Film 'Les Amants ee Demain'*: Les amants de demain; Les neiges de Finlande; Fais comme si; Tant qu'il y aura des jours.
ESRF 1215:	C'est un homme terrible; Je me souviens d'une chanson; Tatave.
ESRF 1245:	Milord; Je sais comment.
ESRF 1262:	Boulevard du Crime; La ville inconnue; La vie l'amour.
ESRF 1289:	Les amants merveilleux; Cri du coeur; C'est l'amour. Cover: Douglas Davies.
ESRF 1292:	Ouragan; Opinion publique; Le vieux piano. Cover: Douglas Davies.
ESRF 1303:	Non, je ne regrette rien; Les mots d'amour; Jérusalem. First pressing. Cover: Leloir.
ESRF 1305:	*Édith Piaf Chante Charles Dumont*: Mon Dieu; Les flons-flons du bal; La belle histoire d'amour. Sleeve notes: Édith Piaf.
ESRF 1306:	Exodus; Marie-Trottoir; Dans leur baiser.
ESRF 1312:	Non, je ne regrette rien; Les mots d'amour; Toujours aimer, Mon vieux Lucien. Second pressing. Cover: Levin.
ESRF 1319:	*Édith Piaf et Charles Dumont Chantent l'Amour*: Les amants; C'est peut-être ça; La fille qui pleurait dans la rue. (The latter sung by Dumont).
ESRF 1357:	*Chansons à la Une*: Toi tu l'entends pas; Ca fait drôle; Fallait-il; Polichnelle.

ESRF 1361:   Emporte-moi; Le petit brouillard; Musique à tout va; À quoi ça sert l'amour?

ESRF 1373:   Le droit d'aimer; Le rendez-vous; Roulez tambours.

ESRF 1466:   *Édith Piaf Avec Les Compagnons de la Chanson*: Les trois cloches; Dans les Prisons de Nantes; Le roi a fait battre tambour; Céline.

ESRF 1921:   L'homme de Berlin; Traqué; Le diable de la Bastille; Les gens.

Édith PIAF LONG PLAY

FS 1008:   La vie en rose; C'est d'la faute à tes yeux; La fête continue; Hymne à l'amour; Je hais les dimanches; Padam padam; Plus bleus que tes yeux; Jézébel.

FS 1021:   *Le bel indifférent*. With Jacques Pills.

FS 1037:   Soeur Anne; Heureuse; N'y vas pas Manuel; Et moi; Les amants de Venise; La goualante du pauvre Jean; Johnny tu n'est pas un ange; Le 'ça ira'; Bravo pour le Clown; L'éffet que tu me fais.

FS 1049:   *Édith Piaf à l'Olympia Numéro I*: Heureuse; Avec ce soleil; C'est à Hambourg; Légende; Enfin le printemps; Miséricorde; Je t'ai dans la peau; La goualante du pauvre Jean; Bravo pour le clown; Padam padam.

FS1065:   *Édith Piaf à l'Olympia Numéro 2*: Marie La Française; Une dame; L'homme à la moto; Toi qui sais; Hymne à l'amour; Les amants d'un jour; Bravo pour le clown; L'accordéoniste.

FS 1075:   *Édith Piaf à l'Olympia Numero 3*: Comme moi; Salle d'attente; Les prisons du roi; La foule; Les grognards; Mon manège à moi; Bravo pour le clown; Hymne à l'amour.

FS 1083:   *Huit Chansons Nouvelles*: C'est l'amour; Ouragan; T'es beau tu sais; Cri du Coeur; Le vieux piano; Les amants merveilleux; Je suis à toi; Opinion publique.

FS 1103:   Le billard électrique; Faut pas qu'il se figure; Carmen's Story; Qu'il était triste cet anglais.

FS 1104:   Les amants de Téruel; Quatorze juillet; Toi tu l'entends pas; Polichinelle; Ça fait drôle; On cherche un auguste; Une valse; Fallait-il.

THÉO SARAPO EXTENDED PLAY

ESRF 1366:   Pour qui tu prends (Piaf, Lai); Départ (Piaf, Lai); Chez Sabine (Piaf, Véran).

ESRF 1374:   Les enfants de la mode; Pense à moi; Les mains; Garce de vie (All written by Piaf, Lai).

ESRF 1383:   Un dimanche à Londres (Piaf, Véran); La bande en noir (Piaf, Véran); A l'aube (Piaf-Lai); Les rebelles (Vendome, Véran).

ESRF 1393:   Chanson d'amour d'aujourd'hui (Piaf, Lai); Bluff! (Piaf, Lai); Ce jour viendra (Delanoe, Denoncin); Pourquoi je l'aime (Raya, Maine).

ESRF 1450:   La maison qui ne chante plus (Gall, Commaret); Les filles c'est comme ça (Berney, Fontenoy, Kesslair); J'ai laissé (Nencioli, Revaux); La vie continue (Delanoe, Stanrey).

ESRF 1711:   Tu as changé (Faure, Similel); Comme Al Capone (Commaret, Carriere); Nous n'étions pas pareils (Moustaki); Les autres (Commaret, Vendome).

ESRF 1771:   Le jour où tu sauras (Fontane); La solitude (Commaret-Carriere); Le coeur au Soleil (Commaret-Carriere); New York (Commaret-Carriere).

ESRF 1851:   L'age ingrat; Dis-moi Alice; Je préfère aller au cinéma; Les amours sans issus (All written by Commaret, Sarapo).

SCRF 627:   Les rebelles; La bande en noir.

ESRF 1906:   Tous mes chemins (Sarapo, Commaret); Sainte Sarah (Aznavoir, Dimay); Quand (Sarapo, Commaret); Si moi je t'aime (Baschung, Dousset).

CO16-10056   Les aventuriers (Roubaix, Lang); Dans la nuit (Senlis, Delécluse, Lai); Oui je veux vivre (Dona, Demarny); À tort ou à raison (Dona-Nyel).

INDEX OF NAMES

■ ■ ■